Illustrator:
Agi Palinay
Johanna Hornbostel

Editor:
Dona Herweck Rice

Editorial Project Manager:
Evan D. Forbes, M.S. Ed.

Editor-in-Chief:
Sharon Coan, M.S. Ed.

Cover Artist:
Keith Vasconcelles

Art Director:
Elayne Roberts

Product Manager:
Phil Garcia

Imaging:
Hillary Merriman

Contributions and Research:
Johanna Hornbostel

Publishers:
Rachelle Cracchiolo, M.S. Ed.
Mary Dupuy Smith, M.S. Ed.

World Geography

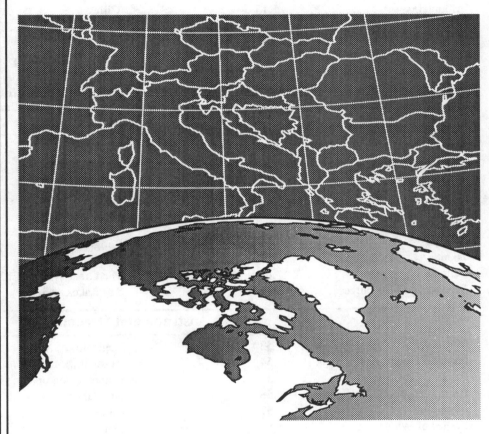

Author:
Richard Rayburn

Teacher Created Ma[...]
P.O. Box 1[...]
Huntington Beach, CA 92647
ISBN-1-55734-471-X

©1995 Teacher Created Materials, Inc.

Made in U.S.A.

Teacher Created Materials

Table of Contents

Table of Contents *(cont.)*

Before You Begin

Introduction

World Geography is designed to help students acquire basic knowledge about each continent. The pages within this book include reproducible maps of the world, continents, and oceans. In addition, informative profiles of the continents and related activities are provided to help reinforce and enhance your students' knowledge of world geography.

Unit Organization and Management

The study of world geography presented in this book is divided by continent.

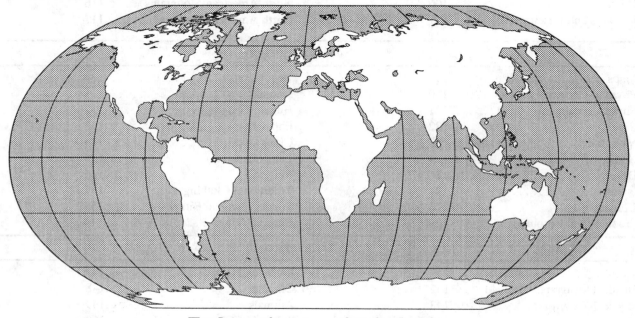

Each continent section includes:

- an outline map and a physical map of the continent
- an information page about the physical geography of the continent
- activities for the study of the physical geography of the continent
- an information page about the human geography of the continent
- activities for the study of the human geography of the continent

Except for the section about Antarctica, each section is identical in format but includes content tailored to the continent. For example, each section includes a population graphing exercise with identical instructions and layout but with data pertaining to the continent. This arrangement provides the following options:

- A different continent may be assigned to each of seven small groups, each group doing the same tasks for its own continent.
- A different continent may be assigned to each member of a group; individuals may help one another with required skills but not the content.
- All the worksheets of one type may be assigned to a group.
- Appropriate exercises may be used with the whole class.

Before You Begin *(cont.)*

Geography Game

The geography game found on pages 152–160 provides students with an enjoyable way of reviewing the information they learned while studying the continents. You may wish to use the geography game as a culminating activity for *World Geography*.

Idea Bank, Resources, and Bibliography

The idea bank on pages 161–162 includes additional suggestions for using maps and activities that extend the unit into other areas of the curriculum.

Suggested resources and a bibliography for each continent are provided on pages 174–176.

Enlarging Maps

If you wish to enlarge the maps provided in this book, here are three easy ways of doing so.

Method 1

1. Use an opaque projector to project the continent outline onto a large piece of heavy paper.
2. Trace the projected lines with a thick black marker.
3. Color, label, and display as desired.

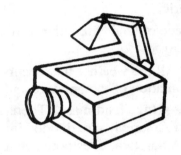

Method 2

1. Enlarge a content outline, using a copy machine equipped with an enlargement capability.
2. Select the desired enlargement size.
3. Choose the paper size appropriate for the enlargement.
4. Print out the enlarged copy.
5. Color, label, and display as desired.

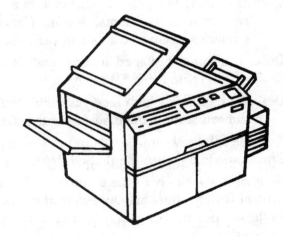

Method 3

1. Obtain a sheet of transparency film.
2. Make a photocopy of the map.
3. Place the copy under the film, being sure that the notch is in the upper right-hand corner.
4. Insert the film and copy with the film on top into a thermal copier after adjusting the exposure setting.
5. Use the transparency for instruction or to create an enlargement.

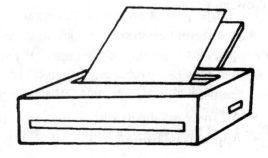

Basic Geography Vocabulary

Hundreds of terms are used in the study of geography. This is a list of basic terms, their definitions, and examples with their locations (when appropriate).

Archipelago—Islands clustered together (Aegean Archipelago, Europe).

Arctic Circle—Imaginary line about 66 degrees north of the equator. North of this line the climate is very cold and harsh.

Atoll—Coral reef enclosing a lagoon (Gilbert Islands, Oceania).

   1. Area of land that is lower than the surrounding land (Great Basin, North America). 2. Area drained by a river system (Amazon Basin, South America).

Bay—Area of an ocean, sea, lake, etc., that extends into the land. Bays are usually smaller than gulfs (San Francisco Bay, North America).

Canyon—Deep, narrow, steep-sided valley, often with a river on its floor (Grand Canyon, North America).

Cape—Piece of land extending beyond the rest of the shoreline into the ocean (Cape of Good Hope, Africa).

Climate—All the weather that occurs in an area over a long period of time. It is usually described as a combination of temperature and precipitation.

Continent—Huge land mass. There are seven continents. Five—Africa, Asia, Europe, and North and South America—are divided into countries. One, Australia, is a continent and a country. The last, Antarctica, does not have any permanent inhabitants.

Country—Any independent nation with a name and boundary. Except for Australia, countries are smaller than continents. Russia, Canada, China, and the United States are the world's largest countries in area. China and India are the largest countries in population.

Delta—Triangular-shaped area of small islands of sediment that divide a river into smaller parts at its mouth (Nile River Delta, Africa).

Desert—Dry area which receives such a small amount of precipitation that little or no plant or animal life can survive there permanently. Deserts may be very hot (Sahara, Africa) or very cold (Antarctica).

Equator—Imaginary line that circles Earth halfway between the poles.

Geography— Study of the features of the earth and of the places where plants and animals live and how they affect and are affected by their environments.

Glacier—Huge mass of slowly moving ice (Malaspina Glacier, North America).

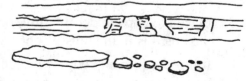

Gulf—Large part of an ocean that extends into the land. A gulf is usually larger than a bay (Persian Gulf, Asia).

Hemisphere—One half of the earth. When divided at the equator, the two halves are the Northern and Southern Hemispheres. When divided from pole to pole, the two halves are the Eastern Hemisphere (Africa, Asia, Australia, Europe) and the Western Hemisphere (North and South America).

Hill—Land that rises to a summit no more than 1,000 feet (305 m) above the surrounding area.

Basic Geography Vocabulary *(cont.)*

Island—Land completely surrounded by water (Madagascar, Africa).

Isthmus—Narrow neck of land connecting two larger areas of land (Isthmus of Panama connecting North and South America).

Lake—A body of water surrounded by land. Lakes are usually filled with fresh water (Lake Superior, North America).

Mountain—Land that rises higher than hills above surrounding area (Himalayas, Asia).

Mouth—The lower end of a river where it flows into another body of water (Huang Ho at Bo Gulf, Asia).

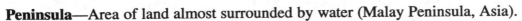

Ocean—Huge area of salt water. The four oceans (Arctic, Atlantic, Indian, Pacific) cover almost three-fourths of the earth's surface.

Peninsula—Area of land almost surrounded by water (Malay Peninsula, Asia).

Plain—Large area of flat or gently rolling, treeless land (Great Plains, North America).

Plateau—Large area of level land that is higher than surrounding land. Plateaus are often cut by canyons, and a mountain system is usually located on at least one edge (Plateau of Tibet, Asia).

Poles—Northern and southernmost points on the earth. The North Pole is on an icecap of the Arctic Ocean and the South Pole is on Antarctica.

Prairie—Flat or rolling land with few trees but covered with grasses.

Precipitation—Rain, hail, sleet, snow, and other types of moisture that fall to earth.

River—Large amount of flowing fresh water (Nile River, Africa).

Savanna—Dry area of flat or rolling land that supports grasses but few trees. Savannas are located in tropical or subtropical areas.

Sea—Part of an ocean that has been identified by geographers as a distinct body of water with its own name (Mediterranean Sea, Europe/Africa).

Steppe—Large area that experiences very hot and very cold temperatures and little precipitation, but supports hardy grasses and other plants.

Strait—Narrow body of water that connects two larger bodies of water (Strait of Gibraltar connecting the Atlantic Ocean and Mediterranean Sea).

Summit—Highest point on a hill or mountain.

Swamp—Area of land that is very wet year round and in which trees and shrubs grow (Everglades, North America).

Tributary—Stream or river that flows into a larger stream or river. A river and its tributaries form a river system (Madeira River, South America).

Tundra—Treeless plain close to or above the Arctic Circle. Some vegetation grows in the topsoil when it thaws in summer, but the subsoil is frozen.

Valley—Long, low-lying area usually located between ranges of hills or mountains (Sacramento Valley, North America).

Volcano—Cone-shaped mountain formed by lava and/or other materials that have erupted from the interior of the earth (Mount Fuji, Asia).

Boundary Map of Africa

Physical Map of Africa

9 #471 World Geography

Physical Geography of Africa

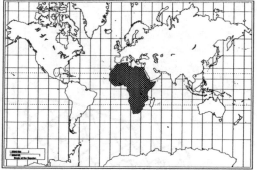

Location: Africa is located in the eastern hemisphere. It is south of Europe and southwest of Asia. It is bordered by the Mediterranean Sea to the north, the Red Sea to the northeast, the Indian Ocean to the east, and the Atlantic Ocean to the west. Approximately two-thirds of the continent is located in the northern hemisphere and a third in the southern hemisphere.

Size: Africa is approximately 11,700,000 square miles (30,300,000 km²) in area, which makes it a little more than three times the size of the United States. It is the second largest continent after Asia. The greatest distance from south to north is about 5,000 miles (8,000 km) and from east to west 4,700 miles (7,600 km). The highest point of the continent is the summit of Mount Kilimanjaro 19,340 ft. (5,895 m). The lowest point is Lake Assal, which is 509 feet (155 m) below sea level.

Climate: The climate throughout Africa is generally warm to hot. In most parts of Africa the difference between day and night temperatures is greater than the difference between summer and winter temperatures.

Precipitation varies greatly on the continent. Most of the heaviest rainfall occurs in central Africa. Snow falls in the higher elevations. In the northern and southern regions, rainfall is limited.

Landforms: Africa is basically a gigantic plateau. The three dominant landforms on this plateau are deserts, grasslands, and tropical rain forests.

The largest and most famous desert in Africa is the Sahara. It extends across northern Africa about 3,500 miles (5,600 km), a distance greater than that between Los Angeles and New York. In the south, the principal deserts are the Namib and Kalahari. Together, deserts cover about two-fifths of Africa.

Grasslands, or savannahs, also cover about two-fifths of Africa. Most of these grasslands are located between desert areas and the tropical rain forests.

Tropical rain forests make up about one-fifth of the continent. The largest area of rain forest is located in central Africa, although some can also be found in the southeast and on the island of Madagascar.

There are two important river basins in Africa. One is along the Nile River in the northeastern corner of the continent. The Nile is the longest river in the world. The other basin is the huge Congo Basin in central Africa, which includes the Congo River and its tributaries.

The longest fresh-water lake in the world, Lake Tanganyika, is located in eastern Africa, as is Lake Victoria, the world's third largest lake.

The major mountain ranges of Africa are in the extreme northwest and in the east. In the northwest are the Atlas Mountains. In the east are many high mountains, including Mount Kilimanjaro, the highest peak in Africa.

Many islands are part of Africa, including one of the largest in the world, Madagascar.

One interesting feature of the continent is the Great Rift Valley. It runs north to south for hundreds of miles (km) in the eastern region of the continent. This feature is actually many steep-sided valleys formed by cracks in the earth's surface.

Name _____ Date _____

Physical Features of Africa

Some major features of Africa are labeled with letters on the map. Match the letters to the names of the features listed below.

_____ 1. Atlas Mountains

_____ 2. Cape of Good Hope

_____ 3. Congo Basin

_____ 4. Ethiopia Highlands

_____ 5. Gulf of Guinea

_____ 6. Kalahari Desert

_____ 7. Lake Victoria

_____ 8. Madagascar

_____ 9. Mediterranean Sea

_____ 10. Mozambique Channel

_____ 11. Niger River

_____ 12. Nile River

_____ 13. Red Sea

_____ 14. Sahara

_____ 15. Somali Peninsula

Name _____   Date _____

Rivers of Africa

Use the clues to help
you match the letters
on the map to the
correct names.

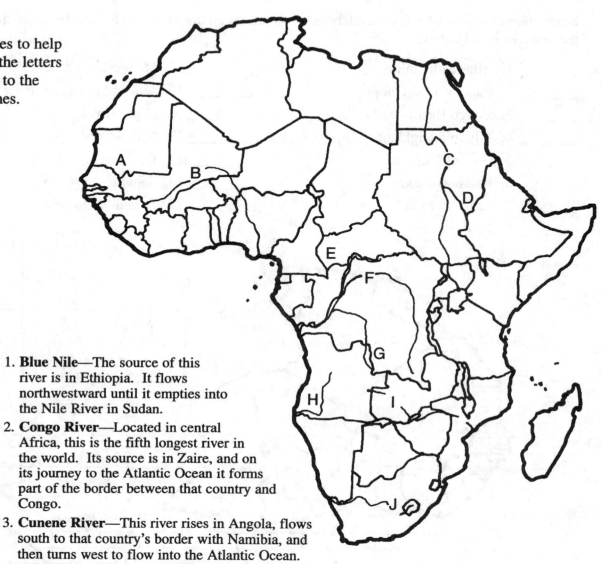

_____ 1. **Blue Nile**—The source of this
river is in Ethiopia. It flows
northwestward until it empties into
the Nile River in Sudan.

_____ 2. **Congo River**—Located in central
Africa, this is the fifth longest river in
the world. Its source is in Zaire, and on
its journey to the Atlantic Ocean it forms
part of the border between that country and
Congo.

_____ 3. **Cunene River**—This river rises in Angola, flows
south to that country's border with Namibia, and
then turns west to flow into the Atlantic Ocean.

_____ 4. **Kasai River**—This river begins in Angola. It does not empty into an ocean. Instead, it flows
through Zaire until it meets the Congo River.

_____ 5. **Niger River**—On its way to the Gulf of Guinea in the Atlantic Ocean, this river flows in a great
loop for about 2,600 miles (4,160 km). Before it reaches the sea, it spreads out to form the
largest delta in Africa.

_____ 6. **Nile River**—This is the longest river in the world. It flows northward for more than 4,100 miles
(6,560 km) through countries in northeast Africa. After spreading out to form a huge delta it
flows into the Mediterranean Sea.

_____ 7. **Orange River**—For most of its journey towards the Atlantic Ocean, this river flows through the
country of South Africa. Its source, however, is in the country of Lesotho.

_____ 8. **Senegal River**—This river rises in the country of Guinea in west Africa. It flows mostly
northwest through Mali and between Mauritania and Senegal.

_____ 9. **Ubangi River**—As it flows towards the Congo River, this river forms the boundary between the
Central African Republic and Zaire and Congo and Zaire.

_____ 10. **Zambezi River**—This river's westward journey is about 1,600 miles (2,560 km) long. Along its
length is beautiful Victoria Falls. It empties into the Mozambique Channel in the Indian Ocean.

Name _____   Date _____

Mountains of Africa

A. Complete the table, using the mountains named in the word bank. Use reference books to find their heights. Then, list them in order by height.

Batu	Elgon	Gughe	Karisimbi	Kenya
Kilimanjaro	Margherita Peak	Meru	Ras Dashan	Toubkal

	Name	Country	Height
1.			
2.			
3.			
4.			
5.			
6.			
7.			
8.			
9.			
10.			

B. Make a vertical bar graph to compare the five tallest mountains.

feet

20,000
19,000
18,000
17,000
16,000
15,000
14,000
13,000
12,000

(mountain names)

Bodies of Water in Africa

Cut out the bodies of water. Glue them in their proper places on the map provided on the next page.

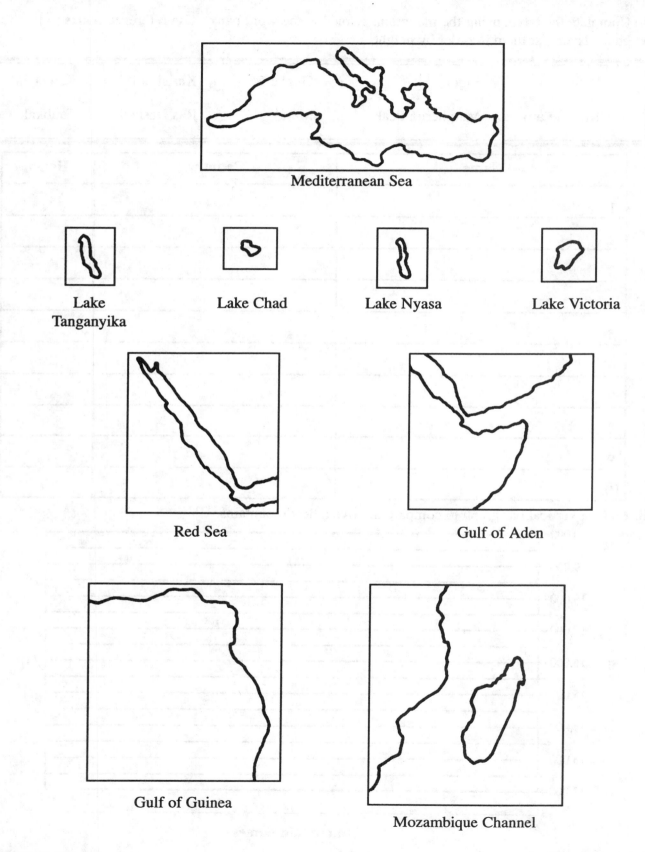

Mediterranean Sea

Lake Tanganyika

Lake Chad

Lake Nyasa

Lake Victoria

Red Sea

Gulf of Aden

Gulf of Guinea

Mozambique Channel

Bodies of Water in Africa *(cont.)*

Glue the cutouts from the previous page onto the map below in their correct locations.

Name _____ Date _____

Deserts of Africa

Research to find out how the following people, places, and things are related to African deserts. Write the connections here. Then, color the desert areas on the map yellow.

1. Bushmen _____
   _____

2. camels _____
   _____

3. ergs _____
   _____

4. Kalahari _____
   _____

5. Namib _____
   _____

6. Nile River _____
   _____
   _____

7. nomads _____
   _____
   _____

8. Sahara _____
   _____

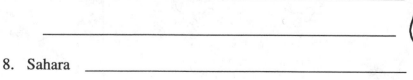

Islands of Africa

Use an atlas to match the latitudes and longitudes of the islands with their names.

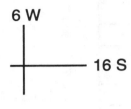

6 W

— 16 S

1. _____

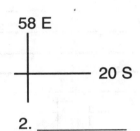

58 E

— 20 S

2. _____

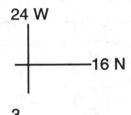

24 W

—16 N

3. _____

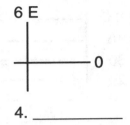

6 E

—0

4. _____

17 W

— 33 N

5. _____

14 W

—8 S

6. _____

57 E

— 21 S

7. _____

56 E

—4 S

8. _____

44 E

— 12 S

9. _____

14 W

—28 N

10. _____

45 E

— 20 S

11. _____

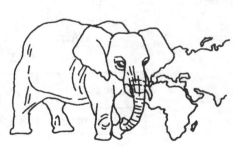

A. Ascension   **D.** Comoros   **G.** Mauritius   **J.** Sao Tome and Principe

B. Canary Islands   **E.** Madagascar   **H.** Reunion   **K.** Seychelles

C. Cape Verde   **F.** Madeira Islands   **I.** Saint Helena

Name_____ Date _____

Climate of Africa

Average Yearly Precipitation

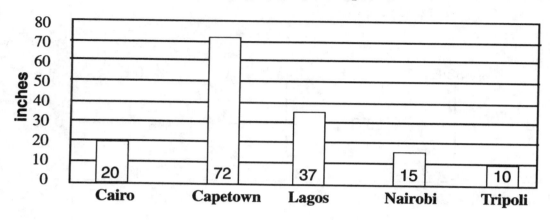

Average January and July Temperatures

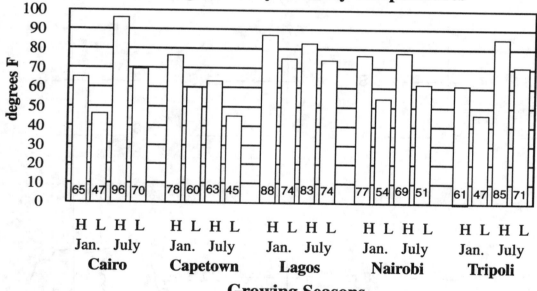

Growing Seasons

Cairo	Capetown	Lagos	Nairobi	Tripoli
12 months	8-12 months	12 months	12 months	12 months

Use the data to determine if the statements are true or false. Rewrite the false statements to make them correct.

_____1. Cairo receives abundant precipitation.

_____2. The difference between January and July high temperatures in Cape Town is about 15 degrees.

_____3. The greatest difference between January and July low temperatures is in Lagos.

_____4. The average precipitation in Lagos is about the same as the average precipitation in the other four cities combined.

_____5. People in all five cities are able to grow crops outdoors in winter.

©1995 Teacher Created Materials, Inc.

Name _____ Date _____

Products and Resources of Africa

Use an encyclopedia and/or atlas to find the information needed to complete the chart. One is given as an example. (Note: Use *agriculture, manufacturing, mining, forestry,* or *fishing* for "Type of Product.")

Product	Leading African Producer	Type of Product	World Rank
cattle	Ethiopia	agriculture	ninth
bananas			
bauxite			
coal			
coffee			
copper			
cotton			
diamonds			
forest products			
manganese			
natural gas			
oranges			
phospate			
uranium			
wool			

Use the information on the chart to answer the questions.

1. How many different countries are listed on your chart?_____

2. Which country is most often listed? _____

3. What type of product is most often listed?_____

4. Which country listed seems to be the wealthiest? _____

   Why? _____

   _____

5. In what parts of Africa are most of these countries located?_____

Name_____ Date _____

Vegetation of Africa

Write one fact about the vegetation that grows in the areas listed below. Lightly shade the correct areas with the colors indicated. Use reference books such as atlases and encyclopedias as sources for this information.

1. Desert (yellow)

    _____

    _____

2. Grassland (steppes, prairies, savannah) (yellow-green)

    _____

    _____

3. Forests (tropical rain forests, broadleaf, needleleaf, and mixed) (green)

    _____

    _____

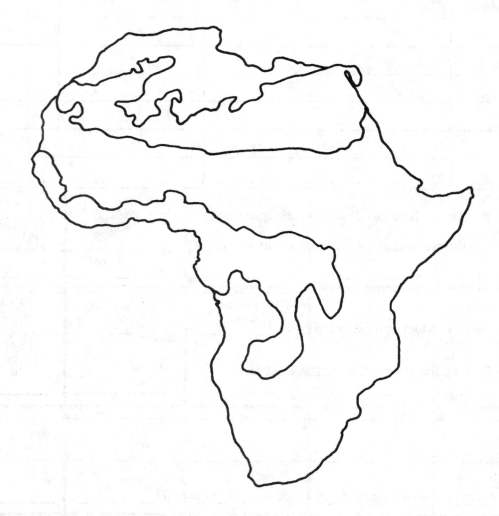

Name _____ Date _____

Animals of Africa

Use reference books to find out about the animals listed below. They can all be found in Africa. In the first column, identify the animal as a *mammal, reptile, bird,* or *fish.* In the second column, write "endangered" if the animal is on the endangered species list. Then, match the animals with their pictures.

1. African chimpanzee _____ _____
2. cheetah _____ _____
3. crocodile _____ _____
4. dromedary _____ _____
5. elephant _____ _____
6. flamingo _____ _____
7. giraffe _____ _____
8. gorilla _____ _____
9. hippopotamus _____ _____
10. jerboa _____ _____
11. lion _____ _____
12. okapi _____ _____
13. ostrich _____ _____
14. rhinoceros _____ _____
15. zebra _____ _____

Human Geography of Africa

Population: As of 1990, about 642 million people live in Africa. Of these, about 500 million live south of the Sahara. Almost three quarters of Africa's population is descended from native African races. About 450 million are black Africans, or Negroes. The others, Pygmies and Khoisan peoples, are not very numerous. The vast majority of these people live south of the Sahara. Most of the population of northern Africa is made up of Arabs (approximately 80 million) and Berbers (approximately 20 million). About 4.5 million people of European ancestry live on the continent, mostly in northern and southern Africa. The 2.5 million people of Madagascar are considered Asian. Asians who live on the mainland are mostly from the country of India, number about 1 million, and live mostly in southern and eastern Africa. Most of the remaining people of Africa are of mixed ancestry.

Lifestyles: About 34% (220 million) of Africa's population lives in cities, suburbs, and large towns. However, this number is increasing rapidly. Still, the vast majority of Africans live in villages in rural areas. Most of these people raise crops and/or livestock. Village people live in small houses that are built according to the environment and tradition. For example, flat-roofed adobe houses are common in northern Africa, while popular southern houses have walls of sundried mud and sloping roofs covered by straws, grass, or leaves. Some rural people are nomadic herders or hunter/gatherers.

The traditional clothing of Africans varies greatly. Northern people wear long, loose-fitting robes or shirts, turbans or skullcaps (men), and long, lightweight dresses and cloaks or shawls (women). In southern Africa traditional clothing includes colorful robes, baggy trousers, turbans, and simple cloaks (men) and long single-piece wrapped dresses (women). Sandals and bare feet are favored over shoes. In all urban areas, western-style clothing is also popular.

The customary diet of Africans varies by region. In northern Africa, for example, foods made from grains, such as flat breads, are basic. South of the Sahara, people traditionally eat one large meal a day which typically includes rice, porridge, or yams. Most Africans do not eat meat often.

Languages: Over 800 different languages are spoken in Africa. Of these, the most widespread are the Bantu, Arabic, Berber, and European languages (English, Afrikaans, French, Portuguese).

Most Africans living south of the Sahara speak one or more Black African languages. Most of these languages belong to the Niger-Kordofanian family. Besides Bantu languages, this family includes Akan, Ibo, and Yoruba. Languages from other families include Dinka and Masai.

Education: Elementary and secondary education is limited in most of Africa. Rapid population growth and poverty are problems for governments trying to build enough schools, and traditional lifestyles make attracting some people to public schools difficult. In Africa north of the Sahara, about a third of the people can read and write. South of the Sahara the rate is about 25 percent. In urban areas the chances for a good education are much better than in the countryside. All major cities in Africa have at least one college or university.

Religious Beliefs: Traditional local religions are the most popular in Africa today with about 200 million followers. There are hundreds of these religions practiced throughout the continent. In general the followers of these religions believe in many gods, although they recognize one god to be supreme. Most also include some form of ancestor worship.

The next most popular religions are Islam and Christianity. Because Islam is so strong in north African countries, they have made it their official religion. Christianity is widespread in sub-Saharan Africa. In some areas Africans have combined it with traditional beliefs.

Name_____ Date _____

Population of Africa

A. Complete the graph, using the information provided.

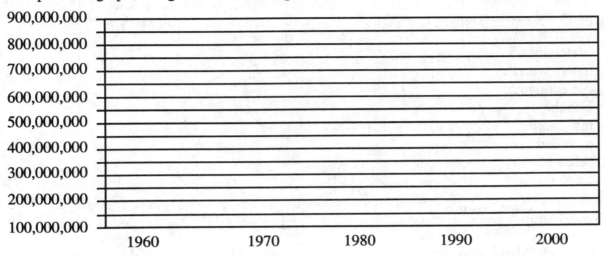

Population Growth in Africa
(rounded to the nearest 5 million)

1. In 1960, Africa's population was about 290 million.
2. By 1970, the population had increased by about 85 million.
3. In 1980, the population had increased by about 115 million.
4. Africa's population in 1990 was about 170 million more than it was in 1980.
5. **Challenge:** Project the population for the next ten-year marker. Enter it on the graph.

B. Complete the graph below with the population data from one African country. Use an encyclopedia or other reference materials.

(name of country)

Name _____ Date _____

Cities of Africa

A. This map of Africa is labeled with letters that mark the locations of important cities. Match these letters with the correct names. Use the information provided below to help.

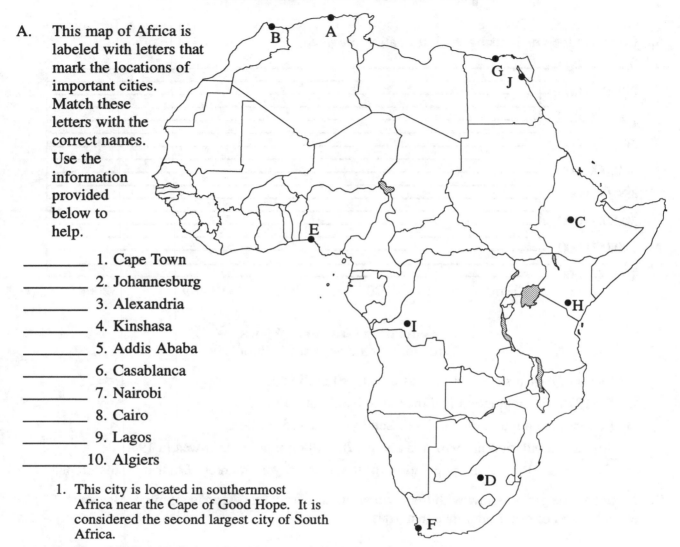

_____ 1. Cape Town

_____ 2. Johannesburg

_____ 3. Alexandria

_____ 4. Kinshasa

_____ 5. Addis Ababa

_____ 6. Casablanca

_____ 7. Nairobi

_____ 8. Cairo

_____ 9. Lagos

_____ 10. Algiers

1. This city is located in southernmost Africa near the Cape of Good Hope. It is considered the second largest city of South Africa.

2. Beneath this city lie many gold mines, the metal that made this South Africa's most important city. It is considered the largest city in South Africa.

3. This is the second largest city and most important port of Egypt. It is famous for its place in the ancient history of Egypt and the Roman Empire.

4. Located along the south bank of the Congo River, this is the largest city of the central African country of Zaire. It is also Zaire's capital.

5. This is the largest city and the capital of Ethiopia. It is famous for its great open-air market, the Mercato, and as an international convention center.

6. One of the major ports of North Africa, this city is the largest in Morocco. It is divided into sections, such as Old Medinah, New Medinah, and Mellah.

7. This is the capital and largest city of Kenya. Among other things, it is famous for a national park located within the city limits.

8. This is the largest city in Africa. It is the capital of Egypt and is located in the northeastern part of the country along the Nile River.

9. Located in western Africa, this is the capital and largest city of Nigeria. It lies on the coast and on four islands in the Gulf of Guinea.

10. This is the largest city and capital of Algeria. The oldest section of the city, the Casbah, is located on a hill.

Name _____ Date _____

Languages of Africa

There are hundreds of languages spoken in Africa. However, most nations have adopted official languages to conduct the business of government. Use reference books such as the encyclopedia to identify the official language or languages of each of the following African countries.

Country   **Official Language(s)**

1. Algeria   _____

2. Angola   _____

3. Cameroon   _____

4. Egypt   _____

5. Ethiopia   _____

6. Ghana   _____

7. Kenya   _____

8. Libya   _____

9. Madagascar   _____

10. Mali   _____

11. Morocco   _____

12. Nigeria   _____

13. South Africa   _____

14. Sudan   _____

15. Tanzania   _____

16. Uganda   _____

17. Zaire   _____

18. Zambia   _____

19. a. List the countries whose official language is Arabic.

_____

b. Are these countries located in north, east, south, or west Africa? _____

20. a. At one time much of Africa was controlled by European nations. People from these nations introduce changes to Africa, including language. How can you tell that some of the nations listed above were once controlled by European countries? _____

_____

b. Which European countries controlled them? _____

_____

Name _____ Date _____

Religions of African Nations

(based on 1993 data)

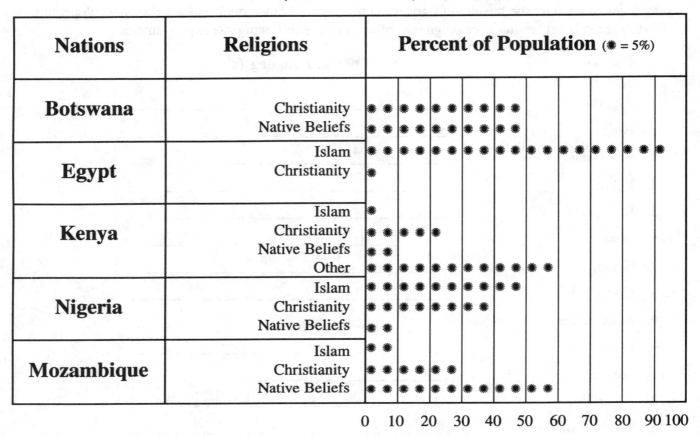

Nations	Religions	Percent of Population (✳ = 5%)
Botswana	Christianity Native Beliefs	
Egypt	Islam Christianity	
Kenya	Islam Christianity Native Beliefs Other	
Nigeria	Islam Christianity Native Beliefs	
Mozambique	Islam Christianity Native Beliefs	

0 10 20 30 40 50 60 70 80 90 100

Use a map and the information on the graph to complete the following.

1. What percentage of the population of Mozambique follows Islam? _____

2. Which country has the largest percentage of Christians?_____

3. What is the difference in percentage between Botswana's and Nigeria's populations that follow native beliefs? _____

4. What religion is probably most popular in nations bordering Egypt?_____

5. Does there appear to be a relationship between region and religion? If so, what is it? _____

   _____

6. Write five additional facts from the information shown on the graph. _____

   a. _____

   b. _____

   c. _____

   d. _____

   e. _____

Name _____ Date _____

Traditional Clothing of Africa

Find photographs or illustrations or make sketches of the traditional costumes worn in three of the countries shown below. On the map, highlight the countries you have chosen. On the back of this page, write a description of each costume. Attach your pictures to this page.

African Masks

Masks have been an important part of African culture for thousands of years. They are very important in all African tribal ceremonies. In dancing ceremonies, for example, people who run the affairs of the tribe wear masks as they call on spirits to keep evil forces away. Many believe that wearing masks of spirits allows the spirits to enter their bodies. They believe they can then become the voices of the spirits. Other times, masks are worn during worship services or in time of danger.

Some African masks are small and worn as ornaments hanging from the neck or attached to clothing. Some are for hiding just the face. Others are headdresses that cover the entire head. The largest masks weigh as much as 80 pounds (36 kg) and hide much of the front of the body.

To make an African mask, follow the directions below.

Materials:

- two pieces 12" x 18" (30 cm x 45 cm) construction paper
- white paper
- transparency
- overhead projector
- pencil
- scissors
- transparent tape
- decorating materials

Directions:

- Find and research examples of African masks. Trace or copy these examples on plain paper.
- Copy the illustrated pattern onto a transparency. Project the image onto the construction paper and trace it.
- Cut out the pattern. Add the dotted lines and V-shapes shown in the illustration below.
- Fold the mask down the middle to make a crease from forehead to chin.
- Wrap the mask around your face. Have a partner mark your eyes, mouth, and nose.
- Overlap the mask at the V-shapes until they meet at the dotted lines. Tape as shown.
- Cut out the eye, mouth, and nose slots. Add features to complete your mask, using construction paper, yarn, paint, or other decorating materials.

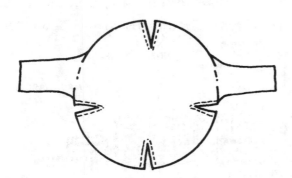

Applications to Other Sections of This Book:

Masks have been worn the world over for thousands of years. Incorporating masks into the study of North and South America, Europe, Asia, and Australia would, therefore, be appropriate.

Reporting About Africa

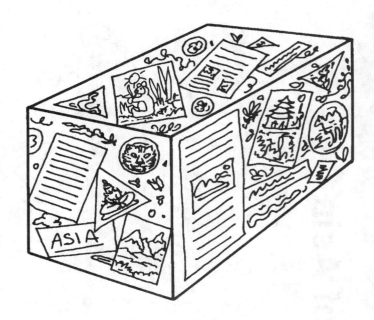

The following directions are for making a container report about Africa.

Materials:

- medium to large cardboard container
- pencil, pen, word processor, or typewriter
- paper (lined, plain, graph, colored)
- coloring tools (pencils, paint, crayons, etc.)
- research materials
- ruler

Directions:

- Choose several African topics about which to research and report. Decide which will be reported in words, charts, pictures, maps, etc.
- Research information about your topics and record the information in the appropriate formats.
- If possible, place items related to Africa inside the container for examination by fellow students.
- Top off your container with an art display appropriate to Africa.

Applications to Other Sections of This Book:

Container reports can be made for any region or topic. If uniform containers are employed by the entire class and nothing is placed on the tops, an impressive display can be created by stacking the completed projects in one area of the room.

Boundary Map of Asia

Physical Map of Asia

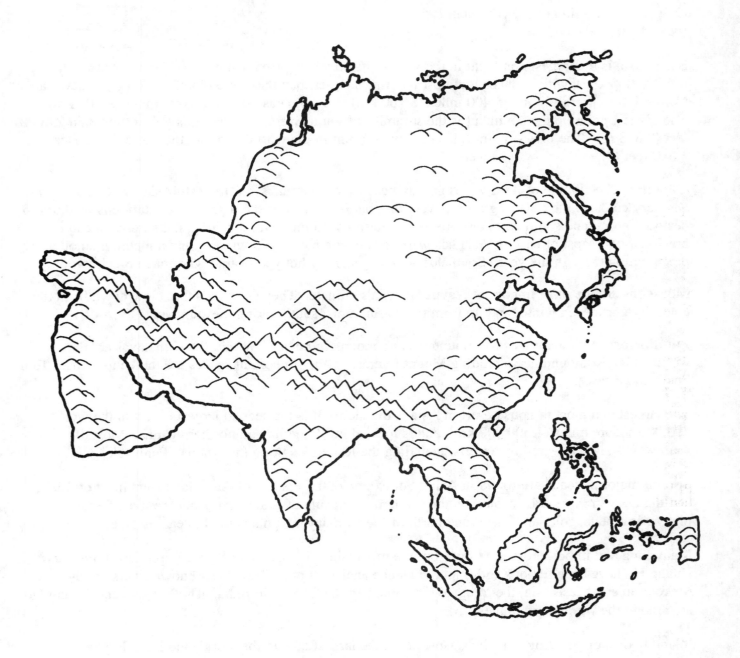

Physical Geography of Asia

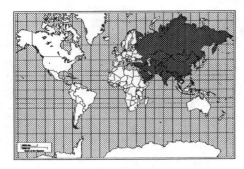

Location: Asia is located in the eastern hemisphere. It is east of Europe and Africa and northwest of Australia. It is bordered by the Red Sea, Mediterranean Sea, Arctic Ocean, Pacific Ocean, and the Indian Ocean. Only a small portion of the continent is located below the equator.

Size: Asia is the largest continent in the world. Its area is approximately 17,000,000 square miles (44,000,000 km²), which makes it almost five times larger than the United States. The greatest distance from south to north is about 5,400 miles (8,700 km) and from east to west, 6,000 miles (9,700 km). The highest point on the continent is the summit of Mount Everest, the world's tallest mountain 29,028 feet (8,848 m). The lowest point (also the lowest point in the world) is along the shore of the Dead Sea 1,310 feet (399 m) below sea level.

Climate: The climate of Asia varies greatly because of its great size. In north Asia, winters are long and very cold. In the polar region it is very dry, but in the rest of the region precipitation is medium to heavy. Central and southwest Asia are mostly desert with mild winters, long, hot summers, and little precipitation. Most of eastern Asia has warm or hot summers, cold winters, and a medium amount of precipitation through the year. Southeast Asia is generally hot year-round with much precipitation.

Monsoons are the most important feature of Asia's climate. They are winds that blow down from the cold, dry north each winter and up from the warm, moist south during the summer.

Landforms: Asia is famous for mountains and mountain ranges. Within the Himalayas are the world's highest mountains, including Mount Everest. Other important ranges are the Hindu Kush, Tien Shan, and Zagros.

The largest and most famous desert in Asia is the Gobi. It is the second largest desert in the world 500,000 square miles (1,300,000 km²) and is located in Mongolia and northern China. Most of southwest Asia is covered by deserts, including the Rub al Khali on the Arabian Peninsula.

Several major plateaus are found in Asia. For example, the Plateau of Anatolia covers most of Turkey, and the Deccan Plateau is located on the southern peninsula of India. Probably the most famous plateau is a huge, cold, and rocky one north of the Himalayas. This is the Plateau of Tibet.

Many long and important rivers flow from the mountains of Asia. The Tigris, Euphrates, Indus, and Huang Ho have been famous and important since ancient times. Other well-known rivers are the Mekong in southeast Asia, the Yangtze in China, and the Ganges in India. The Yangtze and Huang Ho are among the world's ten longest rivers.

Inland bodies of water include the Caspian Sea, the largest lake in the world, and Lake Baykal, the deepest.

Islands are an important feature of Asia, especially in the east and southeast. Borneo, Sumatra, and Honsh are among the ten largest islands in the world.

Physical Features of Asia

Some major features of Asia are labeled with letters on the map. Match the letters to the names of the features listed below.

_____ 1. Arabian Peninsula

_____ 2. Aral Sea

_____ 3. Caspian Sea

_____ 4. Deccan Plateau

_____ 5. Ganges River

_____ 6. Gobi (Desert)

_____ 7. Himalayas

_____ 8. Huang Ho (Yellow River)

_____ 9. Indochina Peninsula

_____ 10. Indus River

_____ 11. Ozero Baykal

_____ 12. Mekong River

_____ 13. Persian Gulf

_____ 14. Plateau of Tibet

_____ 15. Yellow Sea

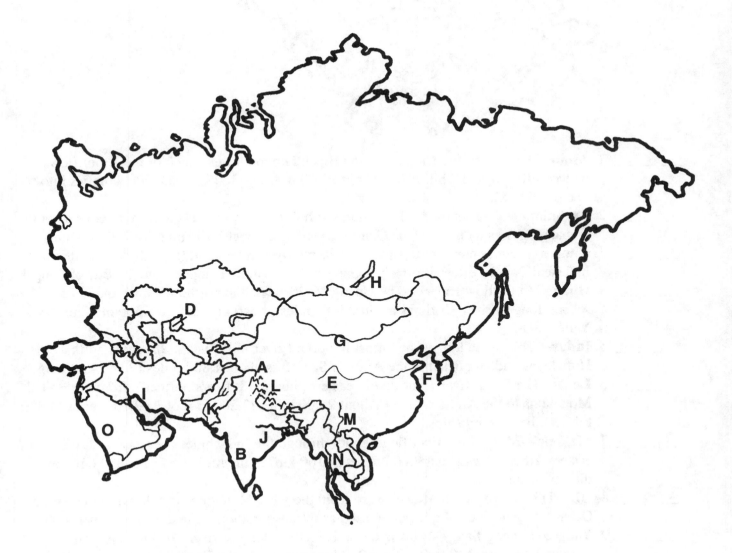

Name _____ Date _____

Rivers of Asia

Use the clues to help you match the letters on the map to the correct names.

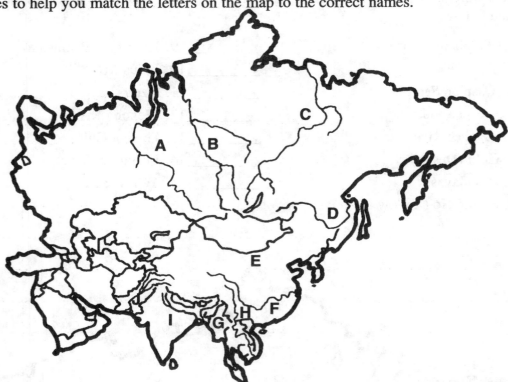

_____ 1. **Amur**—Known by the Chinese as the Black Dragon River, much of the Amur flows
between Russia and China. It is about 2,700 miles (4,320 km) long and empties into the
Sea of Okhotsk.

_____ 2. **Brahmaputra**—This river is located in south Asia. Its source is on the northern side of the
Himalayas as its mouth is at the Ganges Delta. It is about 1,700 miles (2,720 km) long.

_____ 3. **Ganges**—Hindus consider this the most sacred river in India. It flows through northern
India and Bangladesh and forms the Ganges Delta before it empties into the Bay of Bengal.

_____ 4. **Huang Ho** (Yellow River)—The Huang Ho is located in northern China and is its
second longest river. It flows about 2,900 miles (4,640 km) before emptying into the
Yellow Sea.

_____ 5. **Indus**—This is the longest and most important river in Pakistan. It begins north of the
Himalayas and empties into the Arabian Sea. It is about 1,800 miles (2,880 km) long.

_____ 6. **Lena**—The Lena River is located in eastern Siberia. It flows northeast from the Baikal
Mountains to the Arctic Ocean. About 2,000 miles (3,200 km) of its 2,700 miles (4,320
km) can be used by ships.

_____ 7. **Mekong**—Most of the river flows south through the Indochinese peninsula. It begins in
eastern Tibet, flows about 2,600 miles (4,160 km) to the Mekong Delta, and empties
into the China Sea.

_____ 8. **Ob**—This river flows northwestward from the Altai Mountains in Siberia to the Arctic
Ocean. Much of its length can be used as a transportation route during summer months.

_____ 9. **Yangtze** (Chang Jiang)—This is the world's third longest river. It flows eastward
through China on its 3,900 mile (6,240 km) journey to the East China Sea.

_____10. **Yenisey**—This river is located in Siberia. It begins in the Sayan Mountains and flows
northward about 2,500 miles (4,000 km) to the Arctic Ocean.

Name _____ Date _____

Mountains of Asia

A. Complete the table, using the mountains named in the word bank. Use an atlas to find their heights, and then list them in order by height.

| Cho Oyu | Dhaulagiri | Everest | Kanchenjunga | Godwin |
| Lhotse I | Lhotse II | Makalu I | Manaslu I | Nanga Parbat |

Name	Country	Height
1.		
2.		
3.		
4.		
5.		
6.		
7.		
8.		
9.		
10.		

B. Make a vertical bar graph to compare the five tallest mountains.

(mountain names)

Bodies of Water in Asia

Cut out the bodies of water. Glue them in their proper places on the map provided on the next page. You may need an atlas for reference.

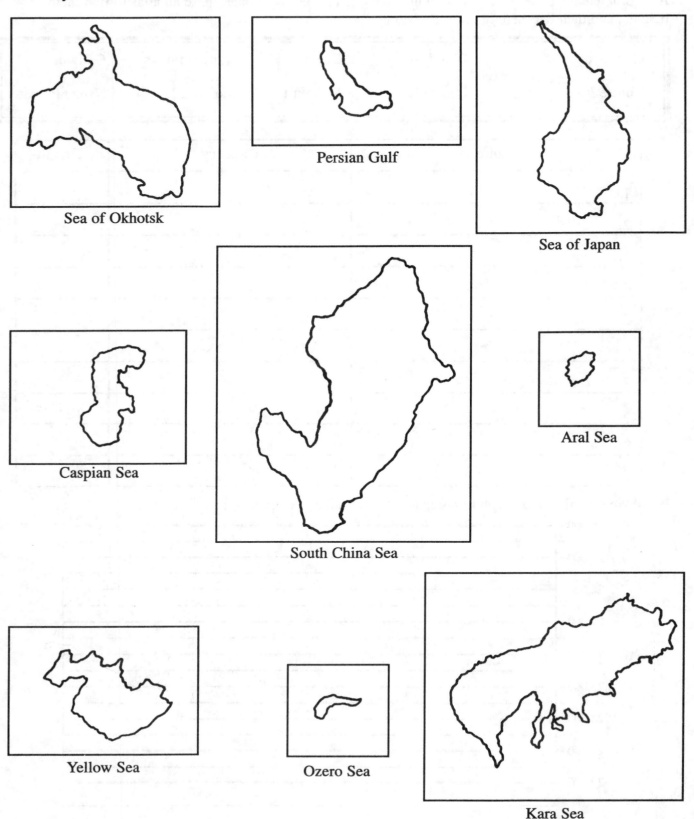

Sea of Okhotsk

Persian Gulf

Sea of Japan

Caspian Sea

South China Sea

Aral Sea

Yellow Sea

Ozero Sea

Kara Sea

Name _____

Bodies of Water in Asia (cont.)

Name _____ Date _____

Deserts of Asia

Describe how the following are related to Asian deserts. Then, color the desert areas on the map yellow.

1. Gobi _____

   _____

2. camels _____

   _____

3. Bedouin _____

   _____

4. Karakum _____

   _____

5. Kyzyl-Kum _____

   _____

6. Rub al Khali _____

   _____

   _____

7. Taklimakan _____

   _____

   _____

8. yurts_____

   _____

   _____

Name _____ Date _____

Islands of Asia

Use an atlas to match the latitudes and longitudes of the islands with their names.

125 E   ── 7 N

1. _____

130 E   ── 33 N

2. _____

143 E   ── 43 N

3. _____

120 E   ── 3 S

4. _____

8 N   ── 81 E

5. _____

122 E   ── 15 N

6. _____

135 E   ── 35 N

7. _____

125 E   ── 9 S

8. _____

110 E   ── 7 S

9. _____

115 E   ── 0

10. _____

60 E   ── 75 N

11. _____

121 E   ── 23 N

12. _____

143 E   ── 50 N

13. _____

110 E   ── 18 N

14. _____

100 E   ── 0

15. _____

A. Luzon   **D.** Java   **G.** Honshu   **J.** Borneo   **M.** Timor

B. Taiwan   **E.** Sumatra   **H.** Sakhalin   **K.** Novaya Zemlya   **N.** Hainan

C. Hokkaido   **F.** Mindanao   **I.** Celebes   **L.** Kyushu   **O.** Sri Lanka

Climate of Asia

Average Yearly Precipitation

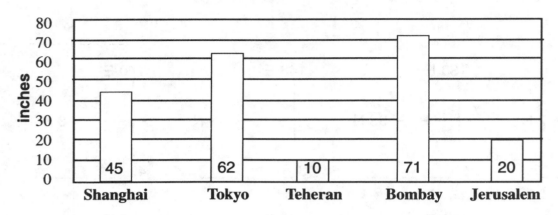

Average January and July Temperatures

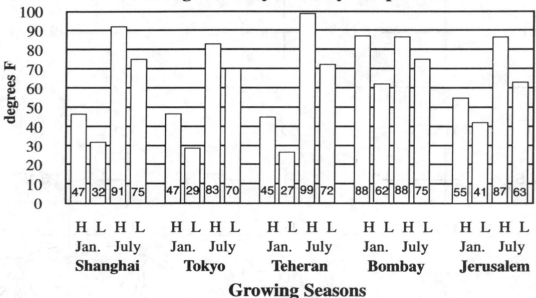

Growing Seasons

Shanghai	Tokyo	Teheran	Bombay	Jerusalem
8 to 12 months	6 to 8 months	3 to 6 months	12 months	12 months

Use the data to determine if the statements are true or false. Rewrite the false statements to make them correct.

_____1. Tokyo and Bombay experience the greatest average precipitation.

_____2. Shanghai experiences the greatest difference between January and July high temperatures.

_____3. The difference between the January and July low temperatures in Jerusalem is about 20 degrees.

_____4. Jerusalem and Bombay have the same growing season because their average precipitation is the same.

_____5. People in all five cities are able to grow crops outdoors in winter.

Name _____   Date _____

Products and Resources of Asia

Use an encyclopedia and/or atlas to find the information needed to complete the chart. One is given as an example. (Note: Use *agriculture, manufacturing, mining, forestry,* or *fishing* for "Type of Product.")

Product	Leading Asian Producer	Type of Product	World Rank
cattle	India	agriculture	first
bananas			
bauxite			
coal			
coffee			
copper			
cotton			
forest products			
iron			
rice			
rubber			
soybeans			
tin			
tuna			
wheat			

Use the information on the chart to answer the questions.

1. How many different countries are listed on your chart? _____

2. Which country is most often listed? _____

3. What type of product is most often listed? _____

4. Which country listed seems to be the wealthiest? _____

    Why? _____

5. In what parts of Asia are most of these countries located? _____

Name _____ Date _____

Vegetation of Asia

Write one fact about the vegetation that grows in the areas listed below. Lightly shade the correct areas with the colors indicated. Use reference books such as atlases and encyclopedias as sources for this information.

1. Desert (yellow)

    _____

    _____

2. Grasslands (steppes, Mediterranean, prairies, savannas) (yellow-green)

    _____

    _____

3. Forests (tropical rain forests, broadleaf, needleleaf, and mixed) (green)

    _____

    _____

4. Tundra (blue-green)

    _____

    _____

5. Ice and snow (year-round) (white)

    _____

    _____

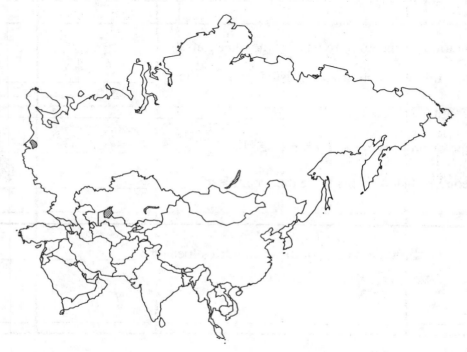

Name _____ Date _____

Animals of Asia

The animals listed below are found in Asia. In the first column identify the animal as a *mammal, reptile, bird,* or *fish*. In the second column, write "endangered" if the animal is on the endangered species list. Then, match five of the animals with their correct pictures.

1. Indian rhinoceros _____ _____
2. Asian elephant _____ _____
3. Bactrian camel _____ _____
4. Bengal tiger _____ _____
5. giant panda _____ _____
6. hornbill _____ _____
7. karakul _____ _____
8. Komodo dragon _____ _____
9. lemming _____ _____
10. Malay tapir _____ _____
11. mongoose _____ _____
12. peacock _____ _____
13. musk deer _____ _____
14. tarsier _____ _____
15. yak _____ _____

Human Geography of Asia

Population: As of 1990, about 3.1 billion people live in Asia. Of this total, about 2 billion (65%) live in China and India. The people of Asia belong to one of three racial groups: European, Indian, or Asian. Members of the European race live primarily in southwest Asia, although many live in northern Asia as well. They account for about 6% of the Asian population. People of the Indian race are concentrated in the countries of India, Pakistan, and Bangladesh in south Asia. They make up about 33% of all Asians. The remaining 60% of the population belong to the Asian race. They live in north, east, and southeast Asia.

Lifestyles: About 70% (2.2 billion) of Asia's population lives in rural areas as farmers, craftsmen, or herders. Shelter, clothing, and diet in rural areas vary from region to region. In southwest Asia, nomadic herders live in tents while farmers live in houses of dried mud and adobe. Usually, rural Arabs wear loose-fitting robes. Common foods include grain products, dates, olives, and fruits. In south Asia, small, closely-packed houses are made of dried bricks or mud. Traditional clothing often includes turbans and garments consisting of one large piece of cloth wrapped around the body. Diets consist of barley, rice, millet, wheat, and vegetables. In southeast Asia, rural houses are usually made of bamboo and wood and are often raised on stilts. Clothing varies from one area to another based on tradition and occupation. Rice, fruits, and vegetables are the most common foods eaten. Most east Asian farmers live in mud or clay brick houses. Men and women commonly wear loose-fitting shirts and pants. Rice, wheat, pork, fruits, and vegetables are important parts of their diet. Many people of rural north Asia live in log houses. Western style clothing is common in this region. Meats, vegetables, and dairy products are part of the diet. In central Asia, many nomadic herders live in skin-covered tents called yurts. Warm clothing and headgear made from the hides and fur of animals are usually worn.

Asia has more cities with populations of one million or more than any other continent. As a comparison, there are ten cities in North America with populations of one million or more, and in Asia there are 72. Most large Asian cities are extremely crowded. Dress and diet are similar to the rural areas, although Western-style clothing is very common.

Languages: Languages from eight of the nine major language families are spoken in Asia. The only family not represented in Asia is the one made up of African languages. In southwest Asia, Arabic is a common language. Hindi is spoken by most people in south Asia. The people of southeast Asia speak a wide variety of languages. In east Asia, Chinese dialects are most popular. In north Asia, most people speak Russian and in central Asia they speak Chinese.

Education: In southwest, south, and central Asia, most people cannot read or write. In southeast and east Asia, education systems vary greatly. In north Asia almost all people receive at least an elementary education.

Religious Beliefs: Asia is the birthplace of all of the world's major religions. In southwest Asia, the major religions are Islam and Judaism. The most popular among people of south Asia is Hinduism. In southeast Asia, most people practice either Buddhism or Islam. East Asians practice Confucianism, Taoism, Shinto, and Buddhism. In north Asia, most people follow either Christianity or Islam. Central Asians are either Buddhists or Moslems.

Name_____ Date _____

Population of Asia

A. Complete the graph, using the information provided.

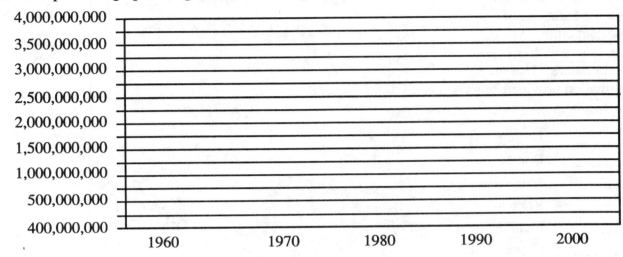

Population Growth in Asia
(rounded to nearest 100 million)

1. In 1960, Asia's population was about 1.7 billion.
2. By 1970, the population had increased by about 400 million.
3. In 1980, the population was about 100 million more than 2.5 billion.
4. Asia's population in 1990 was about 500 million more than it was in 1980.
5. Write one additional fact about Asia's population, based on the graph.
6. **Challenge:** Find the projected population for the next ten-year marker. Enter it on the graph.

B. Complete the graph below with population data about one Asian country. Use an encyclopedia or atlas for reference.

1960   1970   1980   1990

_____
(name of country)

Cities of Asia

This map of Asia is labeled with letters that mark the locations of important cities. Match these letters with the correct names. Use the information provided below to help.

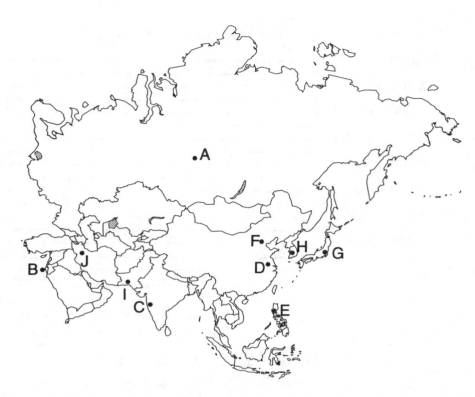

_____ 1. Peking

_____ 2. Bombay

_____ 3. Jerusalem

_____ 4. Karachi

_____ 5. Manila

_____ 6. Novosibirsk

_____ 7. Seoul

_____ 8. Shanghai

_____ 9. Tehran

_____ 10. Tokyo

1. This city is located on the Huang Ho in East Asia. It is the capital of the country of China and is one of the most important and historic cities in the world.

2. This city is the largest of South Asia. It is an island city located on the west coast of the Indian subcontinent. This has helped it become one of India's chief ports.

3. Located in Southwest Asia in the country of Israel, this historic city is about 3,000 years old. It is an important religious symbol for Jews, Christians, and Moslems.

4. Located on the coast of the Arabian Sea in South Asia, this is the largest city in Pakistan. It has a population of about five million.

5. Located on the island of Luzon in Southeast Asia, this is the capital and largest city of the Philippines. It is also the chief port and economic center.

6. This city is located in northern Asia in the country of Russia. It lies on the Ob river and is the largest city in Siberia.

7. One of the world's ten largest cities, this is the capital and economic center of the country of South Korea.

8. This is one of the world's five largest cities. It is located in East Asia near the East China Sea on the Huangpu River. It is the largest city and most important industrial center in China.

9. This city is located on a plateau south of the Caspian Sea in southwest Asia. It is the capital and largest city of Iran.

10. This is the capital of Japan and one of the five largest cities in the world. It is located on the island of Honshu. It is one of the world's great manufacturing and trading centers.

Name _____ Date _____

Languages of Asia

There are hundreds of languages spoken in Asia. However, many nations have adopted official languages to conduct the business of government. Identify the official language or languages of each of the following countries.

Country   **Official Language(s)**

1. Bangladesh   _____
2. Cambodia   _____
3. China   _____
4. India   _____
5. Indonesia   _____
6. Iraq   _____
7. Israel   _____
8. Japan   _____
9. Jordan   _____
10. Korea (North and South)   _____
11. Malaysia   _____
12. Pakistan   _____
13. Philippines   _____
14. Russia   _____
15. Saudi Arabia   _____
16. Syria   _____
17. Thailand   _____
18. Turkey   _____
19. Vietnam   _____
20. a. List the countries whose official language is Arabic.

    _____

    _____

    b. Are these countries located in north, east, south, or west Asia? _____

21. How many languages did you list whose spelling is the same as, or very similar to, the name of the country in which it is spoken? _____

Name_____ Date_____

Religions of Asian Nations

(based on 1993 data)

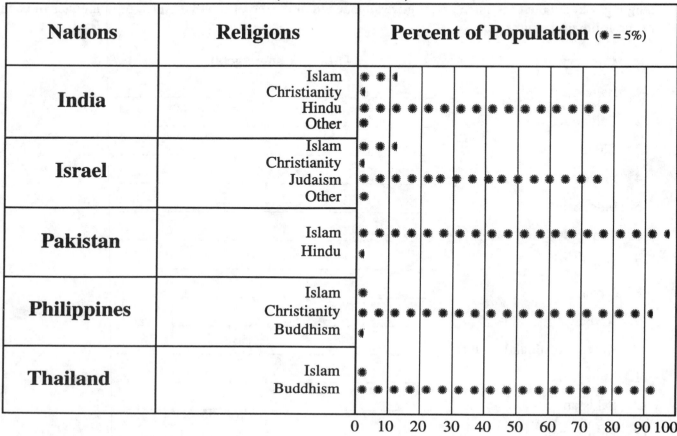

Nations	Religions	Percent of Population (✳ = 5%)
India	Islam Christianity Hindu Other	
Israel	Islam Christianity Judaism Other	
Pakistan	Islam Hindu	
Philippines	Islam Christianity Buddhism	
Thailand	Islam Buddhism	

0 10 20 30 40 50 60 70 80 90 100

Use the information on the graph and a map to complete the following.

1. What percentage of the population of Pakistan follows Islam? _____

2. Which country has the largest Christian population? _____

3. What is the difference in the percentage of Thailand's and Philippine's populations that follow Buddhism?_____

4. India is Pakistan's neighbor to the east. What would you expect the most popular religion of her western neighbors to be? _____

5. Buddhism began in India thousands of years ago. Knowing this, why should you find the information on the graph odd? _____

_____

6. Write three additional facts about the information shown on the graph.

    a. _____

    b. _____

    c. _____

Name _____ Date _____

Traditional Clothing of Asia

Find photographs or illustrations or make sketches of the traditional costumes worn in three of the countries shown below. On the map, highlight the countries you have chosen. On the back of this page, write a description of each costume. Attach your pictures to this page.

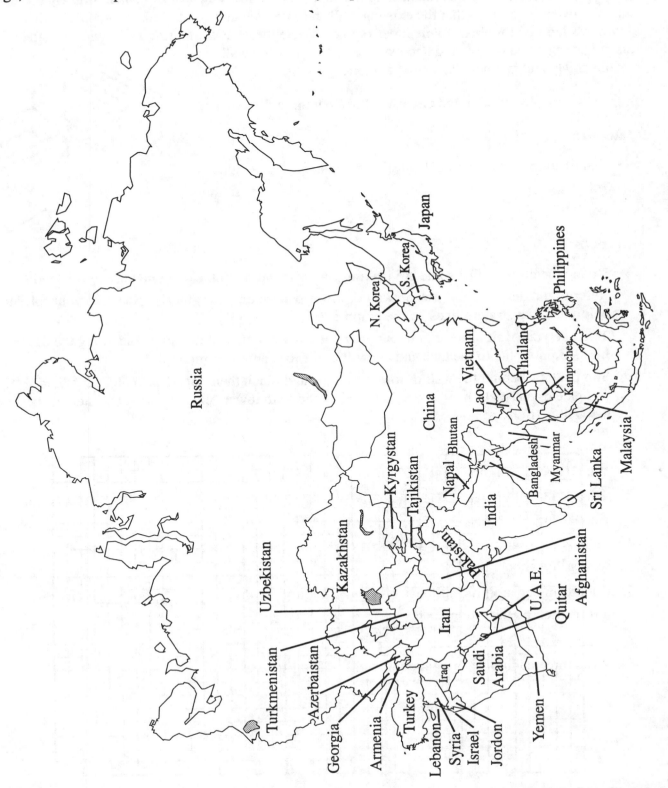

The Great Wall of China

The Great Wall of China is one of the great engineering feats of the ancient world. In ancient times, it was approximately 4,000 miles (6,400 km) long. It actually began as a collection of shorter walls built by independent rulers to protect their kingdoms. When the first emperor of China, Shih Huang-ti, came to power, he ordered that the existing walls be extended and connected. Hundreds of thousands of workers labored for about fourteen years to complete these tasks. During later dynasties, the wall was either neglected or repaired and extended. Much of the wall remains today and is a popular tourist attraction.

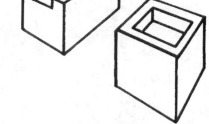

To make a model section of the Great Wall, follow these directions:

Materials:

- manila graph paper with 1/2" (1.25 cm) squares
- ruler
- pencil
- glue
- scissors

Directions:

- Divide the class so that some are making wall sections and others are making tower sections.
- Refer to the diagram to draw the wall or tower pattern on your graph paper. Use your ruler to help you trace straight lines on the graph paper.
- To make your wall or tower, cut out your pattern along the solid lines. Fold along the dashed lines. Apply glue to the tabs and allow it to set for about five minutes.
- Slip the tabs behind the wall or tower sections and pinch them together to attach. When completed, place all the wall sections end to end with towers placed at regular intervals between the wall sections.

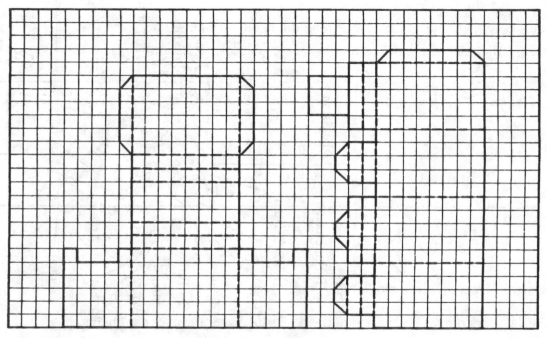

Salt Lakes or Seas?

Three bodies of salt water that lie in Asia are called seas. They are the Caspian Sea, the Aral Sea, and the Dead Sea. The Caspian Sea is bounded by the countries of Iran, Azerbaijan, Russia, Kazakhstan, and Turkmenistan in west-central Asia. Nearby to the east is the Aral Sea, bounded by Kazakhstan and Uzbekistan. The Dead Sea is in southwest Asia between Israel and Jordan. After reading the following facts, decide for yourself whether these bodies of water are seas or lakes.

Definitions:

- lake—a body of water surrounded by land
- sea—a large body of salt water completely or partly surrounded by land

Caspian Sea:

- world's largest inland body of water, 143,630 square miles (373,438 km²)
- 92 feet (27.6 m) below sea level, 3,363 feet (1,008.9 m) deep, and 760 miles (1,216 km) long
- shrinking due to water from feeder rivers being diverted for irrigation
- important source of petroleum and natural gas, less salty than the oceans and has no tides

Aral Sea:

- about 15,500 square miles (40,300 km²)
- 174 feet (52.2 m) above sea level, 220 feet (66 m) deep, and 280 miles (448 km) long
- many islands contained in it
- shrinking due to water from feeder rivers being diverted for irrigation

Dead Sea:

- about 400 square miles (1,040 km²)
- 1,310 feet (393 m) below sea level, 1,312 feet (393.6 m) deep, and 50 miles (80 km) long
- lowest place on the earth's surface
- saltiest body of water in the world (nine times saltier than the ocean)
- contains minerals that are used to make table salt, fertilizer, and drugs

Body of Water	Sea	Lake
Caspian Sea		
Aral Sea		
Dead Sea		

Applications to Other Sections of This Book:

These criteria can certainly be applied to the bodies of water of other continents.

Boundary Map of
Australia and Oceania

Physical Map of
Australia and Oceania

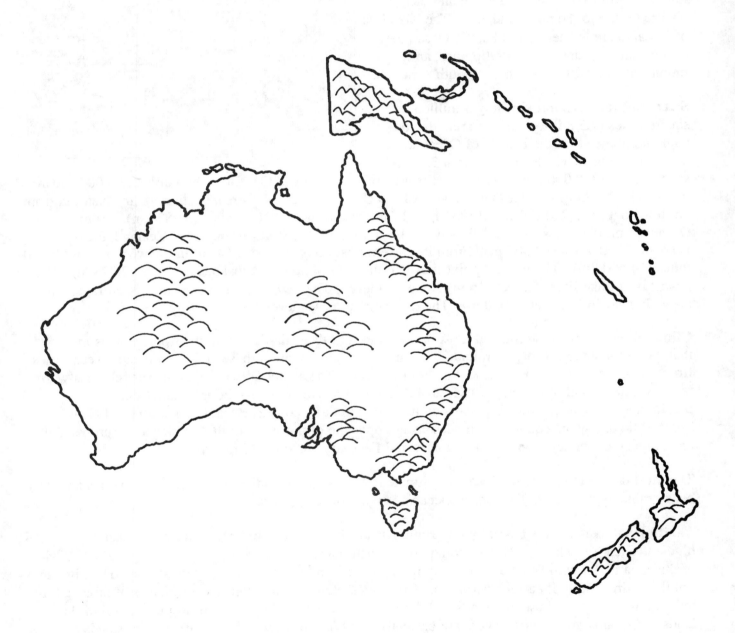

Physical Geography of Australia and Oceania

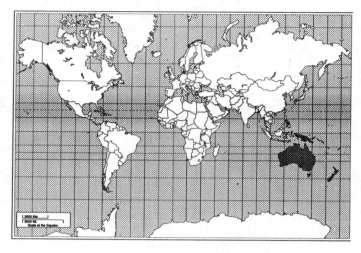

Location: Australia and most of Oceania are located in the eastern hemisphere. Some islands, including the Hawaiian Islands, are located in the western hemisphere. Australia is bounded by the Indian Ocean to the west and south and the Pacific Ocean to the north and east. The islands of Oceania are located in the Pacific Ocean east of the islands of Japan, the Philippines, and Indonesia and west of North and South America.

Size: Australia is approximately 3 million square miles (7.5 million km^2) in area. If you could combine all of the islands of Oceania together, the land area would be about 320,000 square miles (820,000 km^2). Together, the area of Australia and Oceania is still about 200,000 square miles (520,000 km^2) smaller than the area of the United States. The greatest distance in Australia from north to south is 1,950 miles (3,138 km) and from east to west, 2,475 miles (3,983 km). From Oceania's northernmost island, Midway, to the southernmost, South Island, New Zealand, the distance is about 5,000 miles (8,000 km). From its easternmost point to Easter Island in the west is about 9,000 miles (14,400 km). The highest point in Australia is on Mount Kosciusko, 7,310 feet (2,228 m). The lowest is at Lake Eyre, 52 feet (16 m) below sea level. The highest point in Oceania is on Jaya Peak in New Guinea, 16,500 feet (5,030 m). The lowest point is sea level.

Climate: Northern Australia and most of the islands of Oceania lie within the tropics. This means that their climate is warm year round. The amount of precipitation these areas receive in a year varies from a few inches (cm) to about 150 inches (380 cm). The southern two-thirds of Australia has warm to hot summers and mild winters. Most of Australia receives less than 20 inches (51 cm) of precipitation annually. New Zealand's climate is wetter and cooler. Because Australia and New Zealand lie below the equator, their seasons are opposite of those in North America and Europe. July and August are winter months, and January and February are summer months.

The most dramatic feature of Oceania's climate is typhoons. With their extremely high winds and very heavy rains, typhoons are the Pacific Ocean's version of hurricanes.

Landforms: Australia is basically a gigantic island. It has three dominant landforms: deserts, highlands, and grasslands. The western part of Australia is dominated by deserts and grasslands. Most of this area is flat with few trees. Bordering the deserts are great areas of dry grassland. The highlands run the entire length of eastern Australia. This area includes many plateaus and ranges of hills and low mountains. Between these highlands and the Pacific is a narrow band of coastal plains. All of the lands of Oceania are islands. There are basically two types of islands in this area: high islands and low islands. High islands are hilly and/or mountainous. Many high islands contain volcanoes. The largest islands of Oceania are all high islands. Low islands have been created by coral reefs. Most are atolls, coral reefs surrounding a lagoon.

Name _____ Date _____

Physical Features of Australia and New Zealand

Some major features of Australia and New Zealand are labeled with letters on the map. Match the letters to the names of the features listed below.

_____1. Barkly Tableland

_____2. Bass Strait

_____3. Cape York Peninsula

_____4. Darling River

_____5. Great Australian Bight

_____6. Great Barrier Reef

_____7. Great Dividing Range

_____8. Great Sandy Desert

_____9. Great Victoria Desert

_____10. Gulf of Carpentaria

_____11. Kimberley Plateau

_____12. Murray River

_____13. North Cape

_____14. Simpson Desert

_____15. Southern Alps

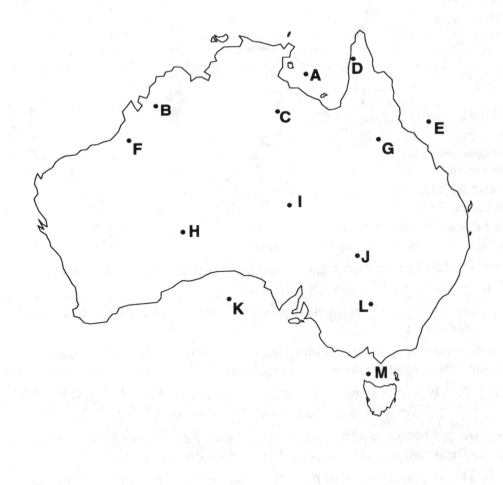

Name _____ Date _____

Rivers, Bays, and Harbors of Australia and Oceania

Use the clues to help you match the letters on the map to the correct names.

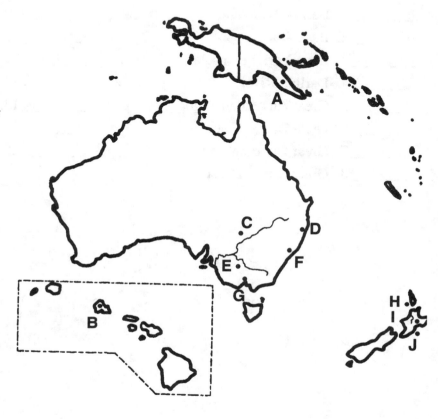

_____ 1. **Botany Bay**—This bay is on the east coast of Australia. It lies about five miles south of the city of Sydney. Captain James Cook gave it its name because of the many plants that grew nearby.

_____ 2. **Darling River**—The Darling is the longest river in Australia. It rises in the Eastern Highlands and flows southward 1,702 miles (2,723 km) until it meets the Murray River.

_____ 3. **Hawke Bay**—This bay in an arm of the Pacific Ocean that is located on the east coast of North Island, New Zealand. It is partly enclosed by Cape Kidnappers and Mahia Peninsula.

_____ 4. **Manukau Harbor**—Manukau Harbor is one of two harbors that serve Auckland, New Zealand. It is located on the west coast of North Island.

_____ 5. **Murray River**—This is the longest permanently flowing river in Australia. It rises in the coast. It is about 1,600 miles (2,560 km) long.

_____ 6. **Pearl Harbor**—Pearl Harbor is a large and important harbor in the Hawaiian Islands. It is part of Oahu Island. The city of Honolulu is located nearby.

_____ 7. **Port Phillip Bay**—This bay is an important port in the country of Australia. It is located in the southeast corner of the continent with the city of Melbourne on its shore.

_____ 8. **Port Moresby**—This is a harbor that lies next to the capital city of Papua New Guinea. It is located on the southeast coast of the island and opens into the Coral Sea.

_____ 9. **Sydney Harbor**—This is one of the finest harbors in the world. It is located on the east coast of Australia next to Sydney, the continent's largest city.

_____ 10. **Waikato River**—The Waikato is the longest river in New Zealand. It rises in the mountains of North Island and flows northward until it empties into the Tasman Sea.

Name _____ Date _____

Mountains of
Australia and Oceania

A. Complete the table, using the mountains named in the word bank. Use reference books to find their heights. Then, list them in order by height.

| Cook | Jaya | Kosciusko | Mandala |
| Mauna Kea | Mauna Loa | Trikora | Wilhelm |

	Name	Country	Height
1.			
2.			
3.			
4.			
5.			
6.			
7.			
8.			

B. Make a vertical bar graph to compare the five tallest mountains.

feet: 16,500 — 16,000 — 15,500 — 15,000 — 14,500 — 14,000 — 13,500 — 13,000 — 12,500

_____   _____   _____   _____   _____

(mountain names)

Bodies of Water in Australia and Oceania

Cut out the bodies of water. Glue them in their proper places on the map provided on the next page. You may need an atlas for reference.

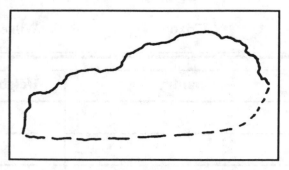
Great Australian Bight

Lakes Eyre, Gairdner, and Torrens

Arafura Sea

Joseph Bonaparte Gulf

Gulf of Carpenteria

Bass Strait

Bodies of Water in
Australia and Oceania *(cont.)*

Glue the cutouts from the previous page onto the map below in their correct locations.

Name _____ Date _____

Deserts of Australia

Research to find out how the following people, places, and animals are related to Australian deserts. Color the desert areas yellow on the map.

1. Simpson Desert _____

   _____

2. Great Victoria Desert _____

   _____

3. Great Sandy Desert _____

   _____

4. Ayers Rock _____

   _____

5. Aborigines _____

   _____

   _____

6. Alice Springs _____

   _____

   _____

7. red kangaroo _____

   _____

   _____

8. outback _____

   _____

   _____

Name _____ Date _____

Islands of Australia and Oceania

Use an atlas to match the latitudes and longitudes of the islands with their names.

157 E

|———— 7 S

1. _____

150 E

|———— 5 S

2. _____

170 E

|————45 S

3. _____

155 W

|————20 N

4. _____

175 E

|———— 40 S

5. _____

172 W

|———— 14 S

6. _____

165 E

|———— 22 S

7. _____

150 W

|———— 17 S

8. _____

178 E

|———— 17 S

9. _____

158 W

|———— 14 S

10. _____

147 E

|———— 42 S

11. _____

140 E

|———— 5 S

12. _____

A. Fiji

B. Hawaii

C. New Britain

D. New Caledonia

E. New Guinea

F. North Island

G. Oahu

H. Solomon Islands

I. South Island

J. Tahiti

K. Tasmania

L. Western Samoa

Name _____ Date _____

Climate of Australia and Oceania

Average Yearly Precipitation

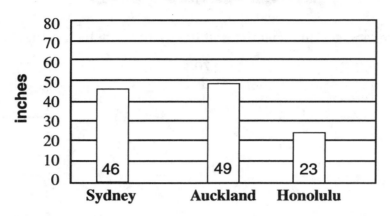

Average January and July Temperatures

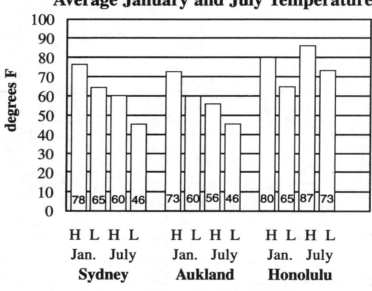

Growing Seasons

Sydney	Auckland	Honolulu
10 to 12 months	10 to 12 months	12 months

Use the data to determine if the statements are true or false. Then, answer the question.

_____1. Honolulu and Sydney experience the greatest average precipitation.

_____2. Sydney experiences the greatest difference between January and July high temperatures.

_____3. The difference between January and July low temperatures in Honolulu is about 10 degrees.

_____4. Sydney and Auckland have the same growing season because they are located in the same country.

5. Why are Sydney and Auckland's July temperatures colder than their January temperatures? _____

Name _____ Date _____

Products and Resources of Australia and Oceania

Use an encyclopedia and/or atlas to find the information needed to complete the chart. One is given as an example. (Note: Use *agriculture, manufacturing, mining, forestry,* or *fishing* for "Type of Product.")

Product	Leading Australia/Oceania Producer	Type of Product	World Rank
wool	Australia	agriculture	1
bauxite			
coal			
coconuts			
copper			
gold			
iron			
nickel			
oats			
silver			
sugar			
tin			
tungsten			
uranium			
wheat			

Use information on the chart to answer the questions.

1. How many different countries are listed on your chart? _____

2. Which country is most often listed? _____

3. What type of product is most often listed? _____

4. Which country listed seems to be the wealthiest? _____

   Why? _____

   _____

5. In what part of the Pacific are most of these countries located? _____

Name _____ Date _____

Vegetation of Australia and Oceania

Write one fact about the vegetation that grows in the areas listed below. Lightly shade the correct areas with the colors indicated. Use reference books such as atlases and encyclopedias as sources for this information.

1. Desert (yellow)

   _____

   _____

2. Grasslands (steppes, prairies, savannas) (yellow-green)

   _____

   _____

3. Forests (tropical rain forests, broadleaf, needleleaf, and mixed) (green)

   _____

   _____

Name _____ Date _____

Animals of Australia and Oceania

The animals listed below are found in Australia and Oceania. In the first column, identify the animal as a *mammal, reptile, bird,* or *fish*. In the second column, write "endangered" if the animal is on the endangered species list. Then, match eight of the animals with their correct pictures.

1. bandicoot   _____   _____

2. budgerigar   _____   _____

3. echidna   _____   _____

4. emu   _____   _____

5. kangaroo   _____   _____

6. kea   _____   _____

7. kiwi   _____   _____

8. koala   _____   _____

9. kookaburra   _____   _____

10. lyrebird   _____   _____

11. platypus   _____   _____

12. dingo   _____   _____

13. Tasmanian devil   _____   _____

14. wallaby   _____   _____

15. wombat   _____   _____

Human Geography of Australia and Oceania

Populations: As of 1990, about 26.5 million people lived in Australia and Oceania. Of these, more than 20.3 million lived in Australia and New Zealand alone. In these countries and Hawaii the majority of the population is descended from Western European or North American immigrants. An increasing percentage of the population in these and other areas of Oceania is made up of Asian immigrants. The native population of Australia and Oceania is divided into several racial groups. Aborigines are descendants of Australian natives. Melanesians are natives of New Guinea, the Solomons, New Caledonia, Fiji, and the other islands in this area of the Pacific. Micronesians make up the native population of the small islands in the northwest region of Oceania. Polynesians are the native people of the islands within a triangular area formed by New Zealand, the Hawaiian Islands, and Easter Island.

Lifestyles: Except for within Hawaii and New Zealand, there are few large towns or cities in Oceania. Instead, most of the population is located in small villages. Usually, native village people live in houses made of wood and thatch. They wear traditional clothing, such as loose-fitting skirts made from cotton, tree bark, or grass. These islanders eat a variety of foods found in local waters and on native plants. Seafood, such as tuna and crab, and tropical fruits, like coconut meat and breadfruit, are popular.

Unlike most of Oceania, Australia has several large urban areas and many towns. In these areas and in the larger towns and cities of Oceania, shelter, clothing, and food are similar or identical to those found in Western countries.

Languages: Thousands of different languages are spoken in Australia and Oceania. Most of these are native languages that developed over thousands of years. During more recent times, foreign nations colonized and/or took control of Australia and the islands of Oceania. When this happened, their languages were introduced and were learned by much of the population. The most widespread non-native language is English. It is the official language of Australia, New Zealand, Hawaii, Fiji, Tonga, and Western Samoa. In some areas of Oceania, islanders speak Japanese or French. On many islands, the people speak a blend of native languages and English. This is often referred to as pidgin English.

Education: Elementary schools are located throughout Australia and Oceania. Fewer areas have high schools, and fewer still have colleges or universities. Many of the elementary and high schools in Oceania are missionary schools operated by Christian organizations. In Australia, many children receive elementary and high school instruction by mail and two-way radios. Colleges and universities are located primarily in Australia, New Zealand, and Hawaii.

Religious Beliefs: The religion practiced by most people living in Australia and Oceania is Christianity. Of the total population of this area (approximately 27 million in 1990), more than 21 million are Christians. The vast majority of the Christian population are members of either Protestant or Roman Catholic sects. Other religions practiced in Australia and Oceania are Islam, Hinduism, and Judaism, although the percentage of the population that adheres to these religions is small. About 3.5 million people of Australia and Oceania are non-religious or atheists. In some regions, people practice native religions that existed before Christianity and other religions were introduced to the population.

Name_____ Date _____

Population of Australia and Oceania

A. Complete the graph, using the information provided.

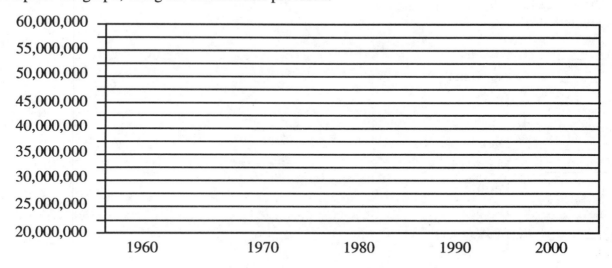

Population Growth in Australia and Oceania
(rounded to the nearest 100 million)

1. In 1960, Australia and Oceania's populations were about 29 million.
2. By 1970, the population had increased by about 5 million.
3. In 1980, the population was about 6 million more than 35 million.
4. Australia and Oceania's population in 1990 was about 5 million more than it was in 1980.
5. Write one additional fact about Australia and Oceania's population, based on the graph.
6. **Challenge:** Find the projected population for the next ten-year marker. Enter it on the graph.

B. Complete the graph below with population data about Australia or one country in Oceania.

1960   1970   1980   1990

_____
(name of country)

Name _____ Date _____

Cities of Australia and Oceania

The map is labeled with letters that mark the locations of important cities. Match these letters with the correct names. Use the information provided below to help.

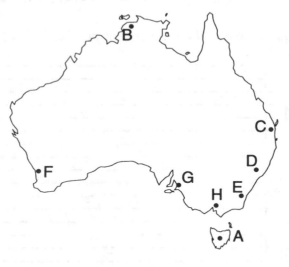

_____ 1. Adelaide

_____ 2. Auckland

_____ 3. Brisbane

_____ 4. Canberra

_____ 5. Darwin

_____ 6. Melbourne

_____ 7. Perth

_____ 8. Hobart

_____ 9. Sydney

_____ 10. Wellington

1. This is the capital and largest city of the state of South Australia. It is located on the southern coast of the country next to the Gulf of St. Vincent.

2. This city is located between Waitemata Harbour and Manukau Harbour on North Island. It is the largest city and chief seaport of New Zealand.

3. This city is located near the Pacific Ocean on the east coast of Australia. It is the capital and largest city of the state of Queensland.

4. This city is located along the Molonglo River in the southeastern region of Australia. It is the nation's capital.

5. This city is named after a famous nineteenth century scientist. It is located on the north coast of Australia. It is the largest city of the Northern Territory.

6. This city is the second largest city in Australia. It lies on Port Phillip Bay on the southeastern coast and is the capital of the state of Victoria.

7. This is the largest city and capital of the state of Western Australia. It is located on the west coast of Australia along the Indian Ocean.

8. This capital city is found on the island-state of Tasmania.

9. This city is located on the east coast of Australia. It is the largest city and most important commercial center of the country.

10. Located on the southern tip of North Island, this city is an important seaport. It is the capital and second largest city of New Zealand.

Name _____ Date _____

Languages of Australia and Oceania

Many languages are spoken in Australia and Oceania. Identify the most commonly spoken language or languages of each of the following countries.

Country   **Official Language(s)**

1. Australia _____

2. Fiji _____

3. Kiribati _____

4. Marshall Islands _____

5. Micronesia _____

6. Nauru _____

7. New Zealand _____

8. Papua New Guinea _____

9. Solomon Islands _____

10. Tonga _____

11. Tuvalu _____

12. Vanuatu _____

13. Western Samoa _____

The following islands are territories without their own governments. On the first line, identify the principal language(s) spoken. On the second line, identify the country that controls the territory.

14. American Samoa

    a. _____

    b. _____

15. New Caledonia

    a. _____

    b. _____

16. Norfolk Island

    a. _____

    b. _____

17. Wallis and Futuna

    a. _____

    b. _____

18. Pitcairn Islands

    a. _____

    b. _____

Name _____ Date _____

Religions of Australia and Oceania

(based on 1993 data)

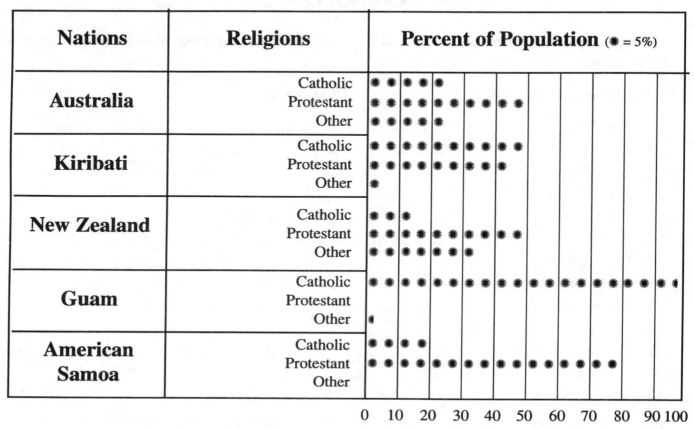

Nations	Religions	Percent of Population (✹ = 5%)										
Australia	Catholic	✹ ✹ ✹ ✹ ✹										
	Protestant	✹ ✹ ✹ ✹ ✹ ✹ ✹ ✹ ✹										
	Other	✹ ✹ ✹ ✹ ✹										
Kiribati	Catholic	✹ ✹ ✹ ✹ ✹ ✹ ✹ ✹ ✹ ✹										
	Protestant	✹ ✹ ✹ ✹ ✹ ✹ ✹ ✹										
	Other	✹										
New Zealand	Catholic	✹ ✹ ✹										
	Protestant	✹ ✹ ✹ ✹ ✹ ✹ ✹ ✹ ✹										
	Other	✹ ✹ ✹ ✹ ✹ ✹ ✹										
Guam	Catholic	✹ ✹ ✹ ✹ ✹ ✹ ✹ ✹ ✹ ✹ ✹ ✹ ✹ ✹ ✹ ✹ ✹ ✹										
	Protestant												
	Other	✹										
American Samoa	Catholic	✹ ✹ ✹ ✹										
	Protestant	✹ ✹ ✹ ✹ ✹ ✹ ✹ ✹ ✹ ✹ ✹ ✹ ✹ ✹ ✹ ✹										
	Other												

0 10 20 30 40 50 60 70 80 90 100

Use the information on the graph and a map to complete the following.

1. a Which country shows the greatest difference between Catholic and Protestant? _____
   b. Which shows the least? _____

2. a. Missionaries flocked to the Pacific Islands to teach Christianity to the native populations. Did they succeed in their mission? _____
   b. How do you know? _____

3. a. Would you expect to find Islam, Buddhism, Hinduism, or Judaism practiced by many people in other countries or territories of Oceania? _____
   b. Why? _____

4. Write three additional facts about the information shown on the graph.
   a. _____
   b. _____
   c. _____

Name_____ Date _____

Traditional Clothing of Australia and Oceania

Find photographs or illustrations or make sketches of the traditional costumes worn in three of the countries shown below. On the map, highlight the countries you have chosen. On the back of this page, write a description of each costume. Attach your pictures to this page.

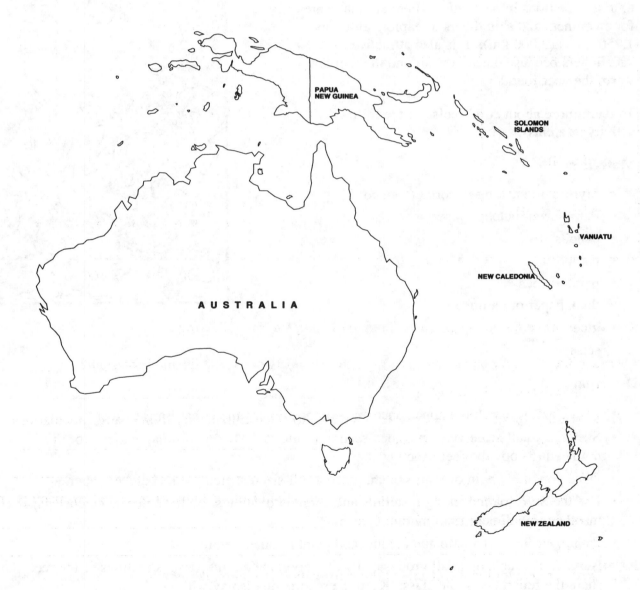

The Great Barrier Reef

The Great Barrier Reef is a chain of thousands of coral reefs and small islands located along the northeast coast of Australia. A coral reef is a limestone formation that lies under or just above the surface of the sea. The coral that forms the reef is made of polyps, the hardened skeletons of dead water animals. Living coral polyps are attached to the reef by the billions. There are about 400 species of these in many shapes and in colors that include blue, green, purple, red, and yellow. Many sea animals also make the Great Barrier Reef their home.

The Great Barrier Reef is one of the most popular tourist attractions in Australia. There are many areas for swimmers and skin divers to explore along its 1,250 miles (2,000 km). It is also attractive to vacationers because the waters around the reef are warm the year round.

To learn more about coral reefs, do the following activity as a class.

Materials:

- Styrofoam packing material ("popcorn")
- mural-sized butcher paper
- pencils
- paints
- paintbrushes
- thick paper or cardboard
- glue
- scissors

Directions:

- As a class, research the appearance and composition of the Great Barrier Reef.
- Sketch a small-scale version of one section of the reef. Use your imaginations for this. You do not need to copy the reef exactly.
- Once you are certain of your sketch, make a full-sized sketch on the butcher paper.
- Use the Styrofoam packing materials and cardboard cutouts to glue onto the butcher paper to make a three-dimensional mural.
- Paint over the Styrofoam and cutouts and paint in other details.

Extension: Individuals or small groups can write reports about the various features of the reef. Orally share the reports with the class. Keep the reports on display with the mural.

Islands, Islands Everywhere

Oceania covers a vast area of the Pacific Ocean. It is not a continent but a collection of tens of thousands of widespread islands. These islands are categorized in two main types, high and low.

High islands are plateaus, hills, mountains, or volcanos that rest on the ocean floor but extend above sea level. They are called high islands because they extend hundreds or thousands of feet above sea level. New Zealand, New Guinea, and Hawaii are high islands.

Low islands are called coral reefs. They are formed from the buildup of millions of skeletons from tiny sea animals. These islands rise only a few feet above sea level. The two types of low islands are coral reefs and atolls. A coral reef grows up around a volcanic island. An atoll often appears to be a group of small islands that form a ring around a large pool of water called a lagoon.

To make a model island, follow the directions below.

Materials:

- large pie plate
- heavy-duty aluminum foil
- dirt, sand, grass, twigs, small rocks, and leaves
- water
- toothpick or pencil
- blue tissue paper, yarn, or plastic wrap
- blue construction paper

Directions:

- Research the islands of Oceania. Choose a type of island for your model.
- Line the pie plate with foil. Remove the foil and re-form it to create bays, inlets, lagoons, and so forth.
- Add dirt and sand inside the foil. Create mountains by raising some areas. Vary the terrain by adding rocks, twigs, leaves, and so forth. Use a toothpick or pencil to carve in rivers and lakes. Add bits of blue paper, yarn, or plastic to give the water color.
- Name the island and write a description of it.

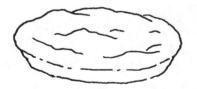

Challenge: Create a topographic map of your island.

Applications to Other Sections of This Book: Study islands of other areas and make models of them that match their specific terrains.

Boundary Map of Europe

Physical Map of Europe

Physical Geography of Europe

Location: Europe is located in the eastern hemisphere. It is west of the continent of Asia and north of the continent of Africa. It is bordered by the Arctic Ocean to the north, the Atlantic Ocean to the west, the Mediterranean Sea and the Black Seas to the south, and the Ural Mountains to the east. The entire continent is located in the northern hemisphere (above the equator).

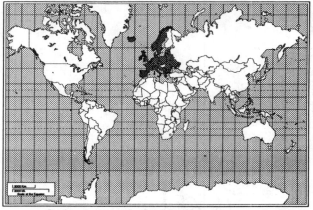

Size: Of the seven continents, Europe ranks sixth in area. Only Australia is smaller. Its total area is 4,066,000 square miles (10,532,000 km²), which makes it about 500,000 square miles (1,300,000 km²) larger than the United States. The greatest north-south distance across the continent is about 3,000 miles (4,800 km). From east to west, the greatest distance is about 4,000 miles (6,400 km). The highest point on the continent is on Mount Elbrus 18,481 feet (5,633 m), and the lowest is on the shore of the Caspian Sea, 92 feet (28 m) below sea level.

Climate: The climate of Europe is generally mild; however, there are areas that get very cold or very hot. Except in the far north and south, summers are usually warm to cool and winters mild to cold. Precipitation is moderate. In the far north, short, cool summers are followed by long, cold winters. In the south, summers are usually hot and dry and winters are mild. Little or moderate precipitation falls annually.

The most important feature of Europe's climate is winds that blow across the continent from the Atlantic Ocean. These winds are warmed by the waters of the Atlantic and help keep the climate mild, even in areas close to the Arctic Circle.

Landforms: Europe is basically a gigantic peninsula that is attached to Asia. Among the important landforms are peninsulas, plains, mountains, islands, and rivers.

Of the many European peninsulas the largest are the Scandinavian, Iberian, Apennine, and Balkan peninsulas and Jutland.

A huge plain stretches across the continent from north-central Europe to the Ural Mountains in Russia. The smaller Great Hungarian Plain is located in the center of eastern Europe.

Most of the mountains of Europe are located in the north and south. Iceland, northern United Kingdom, Norway, and Sweden are mountainous areas. The Iberian Peninsula is dominated by a large plateau bordered by mountains of the Pyrenees. The mountainous Apennine Peninsula extends southward from the Alps. The Carpathian Mountains, the mountains of the Balkan Peninsula, and the Caucasus Mountains cover much of southeast Europe.

Included as part of the continent are thousands of islands. The largest are Great Britain, Ireland, Iceland, Sardinia, and Sicily. Dozens of small islands are clustered in the British Isles, Baltic Sea, and Aegean Sea.

Many important and useful rivers flow across Europe. The longest, the Volga, is located in eastern Europe. The Danube, Don, and Rhine are principal water routes in their regions.

Name _____ Date _____

Physical Features of Europe

Some major features of Europe are labeled with letters on the map. Match the letters to the names of the features listed below.

_____1. Alps

_____2. Balkan Peninsula

_____3. Baltic Sea

_____4. Black Sea

_____5. British Isles

_____6. Carpathian Mountains

_____7. Danube River

_____8. English Channel

_____9. Iberian Peninsula

_____10. Mediterranean Sea

_____11. North Sea

_____12. Pyrenees

_____13. Rhine River

_____14. Ural Mountains

_____15. Volga River

Name_____ Date _____

Rivers of Europe

Use the clues to help you match the letters on the map to the correct rivers.

_____ 1. **Danube**—This river is the second longest on the continent. Its source is in south-western Germany and its mouth is at the Black Sea.

_____ 2. **Dnieper**—Sometimes spelled Dnepr, this river begins near the city of Smolensk in Eastern Europe. It flows southward to the Black Sea.

_____ 3. **Don**—Located in Russia, this river flows southward for over 1,200 miles (1,920 km) to its mouth at the Sea of Azov.

_____ 4. **Elbe**—This river begins in the Czech Republic and flows northward through Germany to the North Sea. It is an important part of Europe's transportation system.

_____ 5. **Po**—This river rises in the Alps and flows eastward through northern Italy. Its mouth is a large delta at the Adriatic Sea.

_____ 6. **Rhine**—Beginning in the Alps, this important river flows northward until it empties into the North Sea. It is one of the world's busiest waterways.

_____ 7. **Rhone**—This river begins at a glacier in Switzerland. It flows southward through France for about 500 miles (800 km) before it empties into the Mediterranean Sea.

_____ 8. **Seine**—The Seine is one of France's most important waterways. On its northwest journey, it passes through the city of Paris and empties into the English Channel.

_____ 9. **Thames**—Pronounced *tehmz,* this is England's most important river. It flows east from south-central England and empties into the North Sea.

_____10. **Volga**—This is the longest river in Europe. It flows southward over 2,100 miles (3,360 km) to the Caspian Sea.

Name_____ Date _____

Mountains of Europe

A. Complete the table, using the mountains named in the word bank. Use reference books to find their heights. Then, list them in order by height.

| Dent Blanche | Dom | Grand Combin | Liskamm | Matterhorn |
| Mont Blanc | Monte Rosa | Nadelhorn | Taschhorn | Weisshorn |

	Name	Country	Height
1.			
2.			
3.			
4.			
5.			
6.			
7.			
8.			
9.			
10.			

B. Make a vertical bar graph to compare the five tallest mountains.

(mountain names)

Bodies of Water in Europe

Cut out the bodies of water. Glue them in their proper places on the map provided on the next page. You may need an atlas for reference.

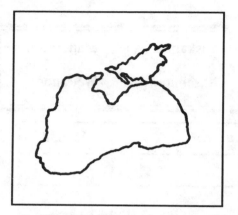

Black Sea/Sea of Azov

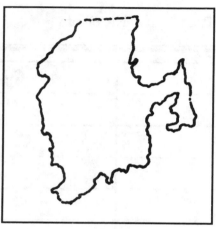

North Sea

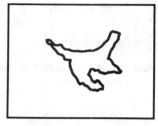

White Sea

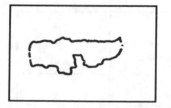

English Channel

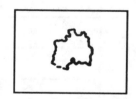

Irish Sea

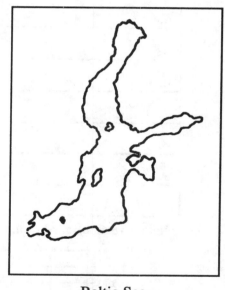

Baltic Sea

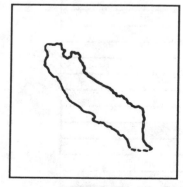

Adriatic Sea

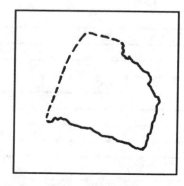

Bay of Biscay

Aegean Sea

Bodies of Water in Europe *(cont.)*

Glue the cutouts from the previous page onto the map in their correct locations.

Name _____ Date _____

The Arid Region of Europe

Describe how the following are related to Europe's arid region. Color the arid region yellow on the map.

1. Astrakhan _____

    _____

2. caviar _____

    _____

3. Caspian Sea _____

    _____

4. Volga River _____

    _____

5. Caspian Depression _____

    _____

    _____

6. Ryn-Peski _____

    _____

    _____

7. Ural River_____

    _____

    _____

8. sturgeon _____

    _____

    _____

Name_____ Date _____

Islands of Europe

Use an atlas to match the latitudes and longitudes of the islands with their names.

7 W
   — 62 N

1. _____

10 E
   — 40 N

2. _____

15 E
   —38 N

3. _____

0
   — 53 N

4. _____

15 E
   — 55 N

5. _____

8 W
   —53 N

6. _____

3 E
   —40 N

7. _____

19 E
   —57 N

8. _____

25 E
   — 35 N

9. _____

14 E
   — 36 N

10. _____

2 W
   — 49 N

11. _____

1 W
   — 60 N

12. _____

18 W
   — 65 N

13. _____

20 E
   — 80 N

14. _____

10 E
   — 43 N

15. _____

A. Balearic   **D.** Corsica   **G.** Gotland   **J.** Ireland   **M.** Shetland

B. Bornholm   **E.** Crete   **H.** Great Britain   **K.** Malta   **N.** Sicily

C. Channel   **F.** Faeroes   **I.** Iceland   **L.** Sardinia   **O.** Spitsbergen

Name _____ Date _____

Climate of Europe

Average Yearly Precipitation

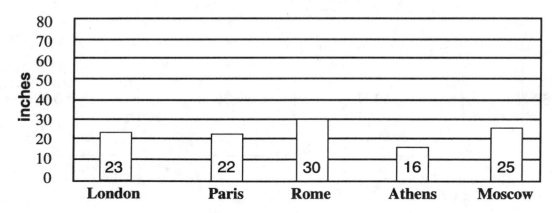

Average January and July Temperatures

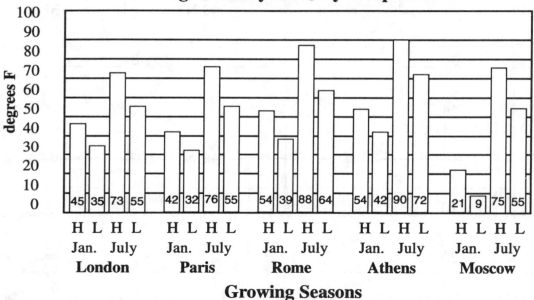

Growing Seasons

London	Paris	Rome	Athens	Moscow
6 to 8 months	6 to 8 months	8 to 12 months	8 to 12 months	3 to 6 months

Use the data to determine if the statements are true or false. Rewrite the false statements to make them correct.

_____ 1. Paris and Athens experience the greatest average precipitation.

_____ 2. London experiences the greatest difference between January and July high temperatures.

_____ 3. The difference between the January and July low temperatures in Moscow is about 46 degrees.

_____ 4. Rome and Athens have the same growing season because their average temperatures are about the same.

_____ 5. People in all five cities are able to grow crops outdoors in winter.

Name _____ Date _____

Products and Resources of Europe

Use an encyclopedia and/or atlas to find the information needed to complete the chart. One is given as an example. (Note: Use *agriculture, manufacturing, mining, forestry,* or *fishing* for "Type of Product.")

Product	Leading European Producer	Type of Product	World Rank
cattle	France	agriculture	10
coal			
copper			
grapes			
iron			
natural gas			
oats			
petroleum			
potatoes			
rye			
sugar beets			
tin			
tungsten			
wheat			

Use information on the chart to answer the questions.

1. How many different countries are listed on your chart? _____

2. Which country is most often listed? _____

3. What type of product is most often listed? _____

4. Which country listed seems to be the wealthiest? _____

   Why? _____

   _____

5. In what part of Europe are most of these countries located? _____

Name _____ Date _____

Vegetation of Europe

Write one fact about the vegetation that grows in the areas listed below. Lightly shade the correct areas with the colors indicated. Use reference books such as atlases and encyclopedias as sources for this information.

1. Deserts (yellow)

   _____

   _____

2. Grasslands (steppe, Mediterranean) (yellow-green)

   _____

   _____

3. Forests (needleleaf, broadleaf, mixed) (green)

   _____

   _____

4. Tundra or heath (blue-green)

   _____

   _____

5. Ice and snow (white)

   _____

   _____

Animals of Europe

The animals listed below are found in Europe. In the first column, identify the animal as a *mammal, reptile, bird,* or *fish.* In the second column, write "endangered" if the animal is on the endangered species list. Match five of the names with the correct pictures.

 1. adder   _____   _____

 2. Alpine ibex   _____   _____

 3. badger   _____   _____

 4. brown bear   _____   _____

 5. egret   _____   _____

 6. hedgehog   _____   _____

 7. herring   _____   _____

 8. mole   _____   _____

 9. puffin   _____   _____

10. reindeer   _____   _____

11. robin   _____   _____

12. roe deer   _____   _____

13. stork (white) _____   _____

14. sturgeon   _____   _____

15. wolf   _____   _____

Human Geography of Europe

Population: As of 1990, the population of Europe was about 700 million. Because it is one of the smaller continents in area, Europe is a very densely populated region. The great majority of Europeans belong to the European racial group. The number of people belonging to African and Asian racial groups is growing but is still small. The European population is divided into many ethnic groups. These groups are made up of people who share the same culture, which includes such things as language or religious beliefs. Some European ethnic groups are Celts, Latins, Germans, Scots, and Czechs.

Lifestyles: About 75% of Europe's population (525 million people) lives in urban areas. The cities and suburbs are very crowded. In most of Europe, city life is similar to city life in the United States and Canada. People live in highrise apartments and houses made of wood, brick, stone, and/or stucco. However, many more older buildings and houses are found in European cities than in American and Canadian ones. Food and clothing are also very similar or identical to what is eaten and worn in the United States and Canada.

In rural areas, most people work in agriculture. Usually farmers live in villages and travel to their land to farm it. In western Europe, much of the farming is done with modern machinery. In eastern Europe there are many places where old-fashioned equipment, such as horse-drawn plows, are used. Generally, the people of the rural areas are poorer than city dwellers.

Languages: Dozens of languages are spoken in Europe. All of these languages belong to the Indo-European language family. Languages from three major groups within the Indo-European family are spoken by most people in Europe. Bulgarian, Czech, Polish, and Russian belong to the Balto-Slavic group. Danish, English, German, and Swedish are Germanic languages. The third group, the Romance languages, includes French, Italian, Romanian, and Spanish.

Education: Most of the people of Europe receive some formal education. Schooling is required by law in all European nations, although the number of years required varies from six to twelve years. More than 90% of the population can read and write. Still, only a small percentage of the population continues into higher education, even though many of the world's oldest and most famous colleges and universities are located in Europe.

Religious Beliefs: Christianity is the most popular religion in Europe. Most European Christians are Roman Catholics. These people live primarily in the southwestern part of the continent. Members of Protestant faiths are concentrated in the northern and central countries, while Eastern Orthodox Christians live primarily in southeastern nations and Russia.

Judaism is practiced by people in every area of Europe, although they do not make up a large percentage of the population. Moslems, followers of Islam, live in Europe but are concentrated on the Balkan Peninsula.

Name _____ Date _____

Population of Europe

A. Complete the graph using the information provided.

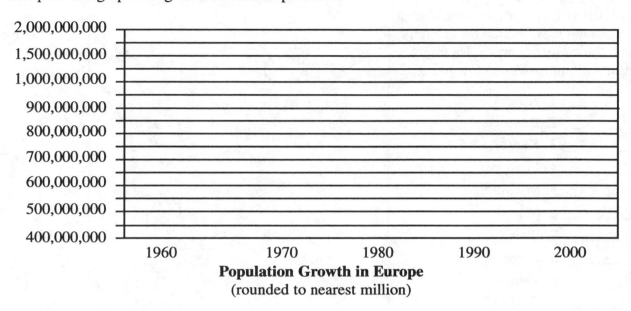

Population Growth in Europe
(rounded to nearest million)

1. In 1960, Europe's population was about 585 million.
2. By 1970, the population had increased by about 60 million.
3. In 1980, the population was about 85 million more than 600 million.
4. Europe's population in 1990 was about 30 million more than it was in 1980.
5. Write one additional fact about Europe's population, based on the graph.
6. **Challenge:** Find the projected population for the next ten-year marker. Enter it on the graph.

B. Complete the graph below with population data about one European country.

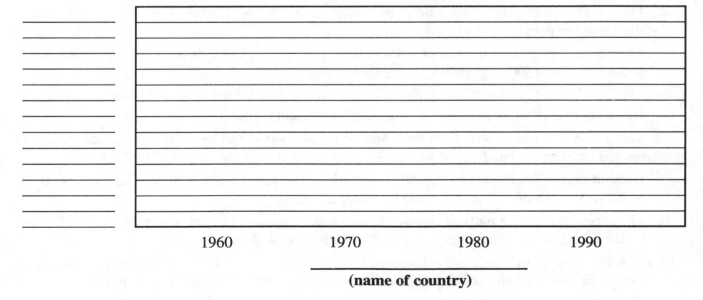

(name of country)

Name _____ Date _____

Cities of Europe

A. This map of Europe is labeled with letters that mark the locations of important cities. Match these letters with the correct names. Use the information provided below to help.

_____ 1. Athens

_____ 2. Bonn

_____ 3. Kiev

_____ 4. London

_____ 5. Madrid

_____ 6. Moscow

_____ 7. Paris

_____ 8. Rome

_____ 9. Vienna

_____ 10. Warsaw

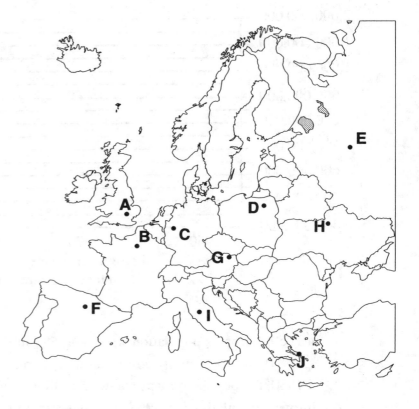

1. This capital city was once the center of an ancient civilization in Greece and the birthplace of democracy. Today it is the capital of Greece, famous for its climate and ancient ruins.

2. Before the two Germanies were united, this city was the capital of West Germany. Today, it is the capital of all Germany. It lies on the Rhine River near the border of Belgium.

3. Once this city was one of the largest and most important in the Soviet Union. Today, it is the capital and largest city of the country of Ukraine.

4. One of the largest cities in the world, this city is located on the Thames River in England. It is the capital of the United Kingdom.

5. Located on a plateau near the center of the Iberian Peninsula, this city has been the capital of Spain since the 1500s. It is also Spain's largest city.

6. This city is the capital and largest city of Russia and one of the ten largest cities in the world. It has many historic sites, such as Saint Basil's Church and the Kremlin.

7. This city is considered one of the most beautiful in the world and has been an important center of art and learning for hundreds of years. Today, it is the capital and largest city of France.

8. Located on the Tiber River on the Italian Peninsula, this historic city is the capital and largest city of Italy. It is famous for its ruins and beautiful fountains.

9. This city was once the musical capital of Europe and the capital of the Austro-Hungarian Empire. Today it is the capital and largest city of Austria in central Europe.

10. This city was almost completely destroyed during World War II. It has been an important city in eastern Europe for hundreds of years and today is the capital and largest city of Poland.

Name _____ Date _____

Languages of Europe

There are dozens of languages spoken in Europe. However, most nations have an official language or one language that is spoken by most citizens. Identify the official or most common language or languages of each of the following European countries.

Country	Official Language(s)
1. Austria	_____
2. Belgium	_____
3. Finland	_____
4. France	_____
5. Germany	_____
6. Greece	_____
7. Italy	_____
8. Lithuania	_____
9. Norway	_____
10. Poland	_____
11. Portugal	_____
12. Romania	_____
13. Russia	_____
14. Spain	_____
15. Sweden	_____
16. Switzerland	_____
17. Ukraine	_____
18. United Kingdom	_____

19. a. Which language appears most often in your list?_____

   b. List the countries in which this language is commonly spoken. _____

   _____

   c. In which region(s) of Europe are these countries located? _____

20. In ancient times, the Romans of the Italian Peninsula conquered most of the people of southern and western Europe. Their language, Latin, became the foundation for the Romance languages. Use reference materials to discover what the Romance languages are and identify them on the lines below.

   _____

   _____

   _____

   _____

Name_____ Date _____

Religions of Europe

(based on 1993 data)

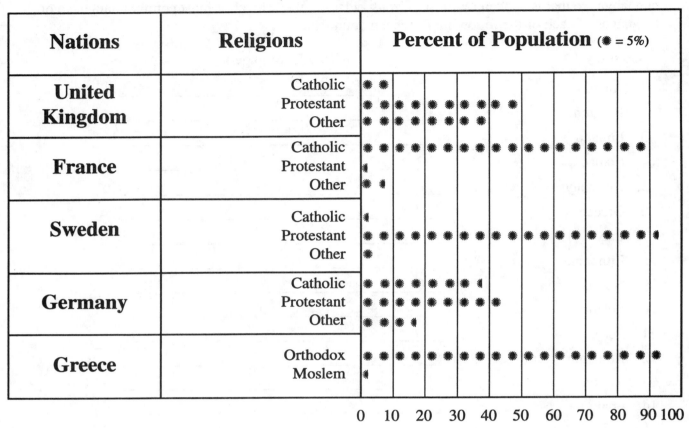

Nations	Religions	Percent of Population (✳ = 5%)
United Kingdom	Catholic Protestant Other	(see graph)
France	Catholic Protestant Other	(see graph)
Sweden	Catholic Protestant Other	(see graph)
Germany	Catholic Protestant Other	(see graph)
Greece	Orthodox Moslem	(see graph)

0 10 20 30 40 50 60 70 80 90 100

Use the information on the graph and a map to complete the following.

1. What percentage of the population of France is Catholic? _____

2. Which country has the most balanced distribution of religions? _____

3. What is the difference in percentage between Protestant populations in Germany and the United Kingdom? _____

4. Spain and Italy are France's neighbors to the south and west. Germany is France's neighbor to the east. What religion do you think is the most popular in Spain and Italy and why?

    _____

    _____

5. Write five additional facts about the information shown on the graph.

    a. _____

    b. _____

    c. _____

    d. _____

    e. _____

Name _____ Date _____

Traditional Clothing of Europe

Find photographs or illustrations or make sketches of the traditional costumes worn in three of the countries shown below. On the map, highlight the countries you have chosen. On the back of this page, write a description of each costume. Attach your pictures to this page.

European Vacation

Millions of people visit Europe each year for business or pleasure. Among these visitors are hundreds of thousands of United States and Canadian citizens. Travel agencies and tourism departments provide people with information to help them decide where to go, how to get there, where to stay, and what to do after they arrive.

To make a European travel poster or brochure, follow the directions given below.

Materials:

- poster board (poster) or paper (brochure)
- colored pencils, markers, crayons, or paints
- scissors
- sources for photos and information (such as printed travel brochures)
- pencil
- ruler
- glue
- pen and paper, typewriter, or word processor

Directions:

- Choose whether you will make a poster or a brochure.
- Gather information about the destination you want to advertise.
- Write an engaging phrase for your poster or an enticing description for your brochure.
- Include pictures of outstanding features, attractions, maps, or other helpful information.

Applications to Other Sections of This Book:

Travel posters and brochures can be made for any area of the world. Futuristic posters and brochures can even be made for other planets.

Flags and Coats of Arms

Flags are an important symbol for a country's land, people, government, and what the nation believes in. Each of the nations of Europe has a national flag which is flown proudly at important times and in important places.

All 43 European national flags are rectangular, although they vary in size. The most common design of these flags (from 20 countries) includes two or three horizontal stripes. Ten flags include two or three vertical stripes. Crosses are prominent on eight flags. Seven basic colors are found on the flags of Europe: red, white, blue, green, yellow, black, and orange. The most popular colors are red (34) and white (30). (For color pictures of flags of Europe and other nations of the world, see *The World Book Encyclopedia*.)

To make a model of a European flag or to create your own flag, follow the directions given below.

Materials:

- construction paper
- colored pencils, paints, markers, or crayons
- source of pictures and information for the flag of your choice
- pencil and ruler

Directions:

- Draw a flag of Europe or make your own design based on the common elements of European flags. Use the following flag terms to guide your design:
- *hoist:* vertical width of the flag
- *fly:* horizontal length of the flag
- *field or ground:* background of the flag
- *canton:* upper corner of the flag next to the staff
- *union:* design that symbolizes unity

Note: The dimensions of European and other flags vary. The fly is anywhere from 1.5 times the hoist to 2 times the hoist.

Boundary Map of North America

Physical Map of North America

Physical Geography of North America

Location: North America is located in the northern hemisphere (above the equator) and the western hemisphere. It is north of the continent of South America and is bordered by the Pacific Ocean to the west, the Arctic Ocean to the north, and the Atlantic Ocean to the east. Traditionally, the southern and southeastern regions of North America are referred to as the Caribbean (island nations in the Caribbean Sea) and Central America (nations south of Mexico).

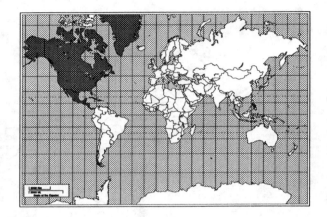

Area: North America is the third largest continent with an area of 9,363,000 square miles (24,249,000 km²). From north to south the greatest distance across the continent is 5,400 miles (8,900 km), and from east to west the greatest distance is 4,000 miles (6,400 km). The highest point in North America in on Mount McKinley, 20,320 feet (6,194 m) above sea level, and the lowest point is in Death Valley, 282 feet (86 m) below sea level.

Climate: The climate of North America varies extremely. In fact, it has every kind of climate existing in the world. Greenland, the largest island in the world, has a permanent ice cap, the temperature remains very cold year round, and the only precipitation is snow. At the other extreme, in Central America there are tropical rain forests with heavy precipitation and hot temperatures all year. Between the northern and southern regions, most of North America has cold winters and warm summers.

Landforms: North America has a great variety of landforms. Among them are plains, mountains, islands, basins, plateaus, great rivers, and large lakes.

Running up the center of North America from the southern United States and into Canada is the Great Plains, a huge, fairly dry area with fertile soil. Along the east and south coasts of the United States are large coastal plains.

High mountains run the length of North America from Alaska to Central America. The greatest of these are the Rocky Mountains in Canada and the United States. On the east coast of the United States is a chain of low mountains called the Appalachians. Along eastern Mexico is a range called the Sierra Madre Oriental.

Most of the islands of North America are clustered above the Arctic Circle and in the Caribbean. Among the northern islands are four of the world's largest: Greenland, Baffin, Ellesmere, and Victoria. The larger islands of the Caribbean are called the Greater Antilles, and the chain of smaller islands is called the Lesser Antilles.

Plateaus and basins are concentrated in the western part of the United States and in north-central Mexico. In the state of Nevada in the United States is a large area of land that is surrounded by higher land. This is the Great Basin. The plateau areas of the continent are cut by canyons. The most spectacular example of this is the Grand Canyon of Arizona.

Many great rivers flow across the United States and Canada. The Mississippi River and its tributaries, which include the Missouri and Ohio, drain a huge area of North America and provide a convenient transportation route into the continent.

The largest freshwater lake in the world, Lake Superior, is among many large lakes that are scattered throughout the north-central area of North America. The Great Lakes are an important source of food and a valuable transportation route.

Name _____ Date _____

Physical Features of North America

Some major features of North America are labeled with letters on the map. Match the letters to the names of the features listed below.

_____ 1. Appalachian Mountains

_____ 2. Caribbean Sea

_____ 3. Florida Peninsula

_____ 4. Great Basin

_____ 5. Great Lakes

_____ 6. Great Plains

_____ 7. Greater Antilles

_____ 8. Gulf of Mexico

_____ 9. Hudson Bay

_____ 10. Isthmus of Panama

_____ 11. Lesser Antilles

_____ 12. Mississippi River

_____ 13. Rio Grande

_____ 14. Rocky Mountains

_____ 15. Yucatan Peninsula

Name _____ Date _____

Rivers of North America

Use the clues to help you match the letters on the map to the correct names.

_____ 1. **Colorado River**—This river's
source is in the Rocky
Mountains. Over the centuries
it has cut deep canyons,
including the Grand Canyon,
on its journey southwestward
to the Gulf of California.

_____ 2. **Columbia River**—Beginning
at Columbia Lake in western
Canada, this river flows 1,200
miles (1,920 km) south and
west before emptying into the
Pacific Ocean between the
states of Washington and
Oregon.

_____ 3. **Mackenzie River**—This is the
longest river in Canada. It
flows northward over 1,000
miles (1,600 km) from the
Great Slave Lakes, past the
Arctic Circle, and into the
Beaufort Sea.

_____ 4. **Mississippi River**—Beginning
in the state of Minnesota, this river flows south for more than 2,300 miles (3,680 km)
before emptying into the Gulf of Mexico. It is the longest river in the United States.

_____ 5. **Missouri River**—This is the second longest river in the United States. It flows east and
south from its source in the northern Rocky Mountains until it meets the Mississippi
near St. Louis.

_____ 6. **Ohio River**—This river is one of the most important transportation routes in North
America. It begins in the city of Pittsburgh and flows westward until it meets the
Mississippi.

_____ 7. **Potomac River**—This river has played an important part in the history of the United
States. On its journey from the Appalachian Mountains to Chesapeake Bay it flows past
Washington, D.C.

_____ 8. **Rio Grande**—This river, whose name means big river, is part of the boundary between
the United States and Mexico. It begins in the Rocky Mountains and empties into the
Gulf of Mexico.

_____ 9. **St. Lawrence River**—This is one of the most important transportation routes in the
world because it connects the Great Lakes with the Atlantic Ocean.

_____ 10. **Yukon River**—This river begins its 2,000 mile (3,200 km) journey in the mountains of
northwest Canada and flows across Alaska before emptying into the Bering Sea.

Name _____ Date _____

Mountains of North America

A. Complete the table, using the mountains named in the word bank. Use reference books to find their heights. Then, list them in order by height.

| Citlaltepec | Foraker | Iztaccihuatl | King | Logan |
| Lucania | McKinley | Popocatepétl | St. Elias | Steele |

	Name	Country	Height
1.			
2.			
3.			
4.			
5.			
6.			
7.			
8.			
9.			
10.			

B. Make a vertical bar graph to compare the five tallest mountains.

feet

21,000
20,000
19,000
18,000
17,000
16,000
15,000
14,000
13,000

_____   _____   _____   _____   _____
(mountain names)

Bodies of Water in North America

Cut out the bodies of water. Glue them in their proper places on the map provided on the next page. You may need an atlas for reference.

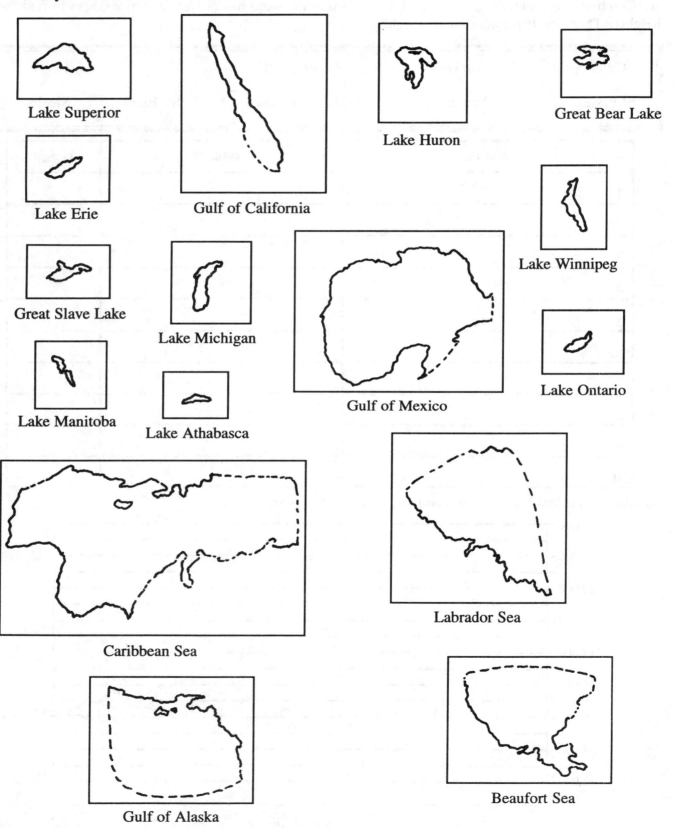

Lake Superior

Lake Erie

Gulf of California

Lake Huron

Great Bear Lake

Lake Winnipeg

Great Slave Lake

Lake Michigan

Gulf of Mexico

Lake Ontario

Lake Manitoba

Lake Athabasca

Caribbean Sea

Labrador Sea

Gulf of Alaska

Beaufort Sea

Bodies of Water in North America
(cont.)

Glue the cutouts from the previous page onto the map below in their correct locations.

Name _____ Date _____

Deserts of North America

Describe how the following are related to North America's deserts. Color the desert areas yellow on the map.

1. Baja, California _____

   _____

2. Colorado River _____

   _____

3. coyote _____

   _____

4. Death Valley _____

   _____

5. Great Basin _____

   _____

   _____

6. Great Salt Lake _____

   _____

   _____

7. Mojave Desert _____

   _____

   _____

8. Painted Desert _____

   _____

   _____

Name_____ Date _____

Islands of North America

Use an atlas to match the latitudes and longitudes of the islands with their names.

85 W
— 75 N

1. _____

78 W
— 27 W

2. _____

100 W
—74 N

3. _____

120 W
— 73 N

4. _____

56 W
— 49 N

5. _____

77 W
— 18 N

6. _____

70 W
— 70 N

7. _____

80 N
— 80 W

8. _____

70 W
— 20 N

9. _____

125 W
— 50 N

10. _____

40 W
— 70 N

11. _____

80 W
— 20 N

12. _____

67 W
— 18 N

13. _____

65 W
— 85 N

14. _____

126 W
— 49 N

15. _____

A. Baffin **D.** Devon **G.** Greenland **J.** Newfoundland **M.** Vancouver

B. Banks **E.** Ellesmere **H.** Hispaniola **K.** Prince of Wales **N.** Victoria

C. Cuba **F.** Grand Bahama **I.** Jamaica **L.** Puerto Rico **O.** Southhampton

Climate of North America

Average Yearly Precipitation

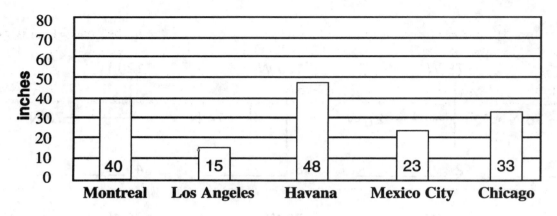

Average January and July Temperatures

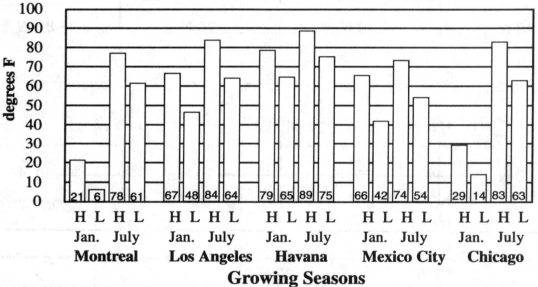

Growing Seasons

Montreal	Los Angeles	Havana	Mexico City	Chicago
3 to 6 months	8 to 12 months	12 months	8 to 12 months	3 to 6 months

Use the data to determine if the statements are true or false. Rewrite the false statements to make them correct.

_____ 1. Havana and Chicago experience the greatest average precipitation.

_____ 2. Montreal experiences the greatest difference between January and July high temperatures.

_____ 3. The difference between the January and July low temperatures in Mexico City is about 10 degrees.

_____ 4. Los Angeles and Mexico City have the same growing season because their average precipitation is similar.

_____ 5. Only people in Chicago are able to grow crops outdoors in winter.

Name _____ Date _____

Products and Resources of North America

Use an encyclopedia and/or atlas to find the information needed to complete the chart. One is given as an example. (Note: Use *agriculture, manufacturing, mining, forestry,* or *fishing* for "Type of Product.")

Product	Leading North American Producer	Type of Product	World Rank
bauxite	Jamaica	mining	4
cattle			
coal			
copper			
cotton			
forest products			
iron			
natural gas			
oats			
oranges			
petroleum			
sugar beets			
tungsten			
uranium			
wheat			

Use information on the chart to answer the questions.

1. How many different countries are listed on your chart? _____

2. Which country is most often listed? _____

3. What type of product is most often listed? _____

4. Which country listed seems to be the wealthiest? _____

   Why? _____

   _____

5. In what parts of North America are most of these countries located? _____

Name_____ Date _____

Vegetation of North America

Write one fact about the vegetation that grows in the areas listed below. Lightly shade the correct areas with the colors indicated. Use reference books such as atlases and encyclopedias as sources for this information.

1. Deserts (yellow)

_____

_____

2. Grasslands (steppe, Mediterranean) (yellow-green)

_____

_____

3. Forests (tropical rain, needleleaf, broadleaf, mixed) (green)

_____

_____

4. Tundra or heath (blue-green)

_____

_____

5. Ice and snow (white)

_____

_____

Name _____ Date _____

Animals of North America

The animals listed below are found in North America. In the first column, identify the animal as a *mammal, reptile, bird,* or *fish.* In the second column, write "endangered" if the animal is on the endangered species list. Match five of the names with the correct pictures.

1. armadillo   _____   _____

2. bald eagle   _____   _____

3. beaver   _____   _____

4. bison   _____   _____

5. caribou   _____   _____

6. green iguana   _____   _____

7. Alaskan brown bear   _____   _____

8. mink   _____   _____

9. moose   _____   _____

10. opossum   _____   _____

11. peccary   _____   _____

12. quetzal   _____   _____

13. sidewinder   _____   _____

14. skunk   _____   _____

15. raccoon   _____   _____

Human Geography of North America

Population: As of 1990, about 418 million people live in North America. Of these, about 245 million live in the United States (59%). Most North Americans are of European ancestry. Of these, most are descended from people of the British Isles (England, Wales, Scotland, Ireland), France, or Spain. A large number of people of African descent live throughout North America but mostly in the United States and the Caribbean Islands. A growing number of Asians live in North America, although their percentage of the population is still small. Native Americans, from Eskimos in the north to tribes in Central America, live in all regions of the continent.

Lifestyles: North America can be considered as being made up of two distinct regions: Canada and the United States, and Middle America. Although lifestyles in the larger urban areas are similar, rural living is very different in the two regions.

Of the 1990 population in Canada and the United States, about 213 million (76%) lived in urban areas. In Middle America, the percentage is smaller (less than 70%). Modern skyscrapers are common in the larger urban areas as are large apartment complexes and housing tracts. All North American urban areas feature modern conveniences, such as elaborate power and water systems, mass media, and mass transit systems. They also have large populations of poor people, most of whom live in blighted or substandard neighborhoods. Automobiles are the most popular form of transportation in most urban areas, although these have contributed greatly to serious pollution problems.

A great majority of people living in the rural areas of Canada and the United States enjoy the same conveniences and services that are found in urban areas. Only a small percentage of this rural population is directly involved in farming. Those who do farm use modern farm equipment to produce a surplus of agricultural products.

The majority of Middle America's rural population is very poor. Most are farmers or farm workers. Few own their own land. Those who do own their own land, raise only enough food for their own use. Most rural Middle Americans do not share the same conveniences and services found in urban areas. Their lifestyle is much as it has been for generations.

Languages: Most people of North America speak English, Spanish, or French. A large majority of Canadians and Americans speak English, although in eastern Canada many people speak French. South of the United States, in Mexico, Central America, and the Caribbean, the dominant language is Spanish. English, French, and Dutch are also spoken in some areas of these regions. Many Native Americans speak the languages of their tribes in addition to the dominant language of the area.

Education: The public and private education systems of Canada and the United States are very large and well attended. Children are required to attend elementary, middle, and secondary levels, and a large number continue into higher education. A vast majority of both populations can read and write. In Middle America, education has improved greatly in recent decades. Still, most people receive only an elementary education. Rural children must often leave school after a short time to help support their families.

Religious Beliefs: In all of North America, the most popular religion is Christianity. However, a majority of Christians living in Canada and the United States are members of Protestant sects, with a large minority that follows the Roman Catholic and Orthodox faiths. In Middle America, a much larger majority are Roman Catholics. Minority religions are, from greatest to smallest memberships, Judaism, Islam, Hinduism, and Buddhism.

Name _____ Date _____

Population of North America

A. Complete the graph, using the information provided.

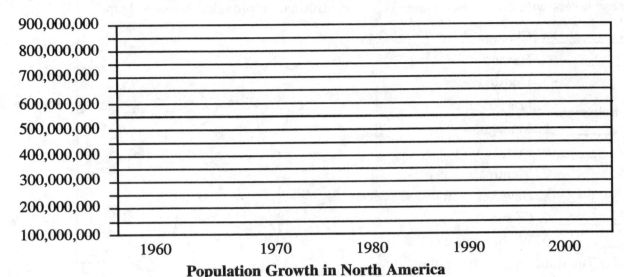

Population Growth in North America
(rounded to nearest 5 million)

1. In 1960, North America's population was about 270 million.
2. By 1970, the population had increased by about 50 million.
3. In 1980, the population was about 25 million more than 350 million.
4. North America's population in 1990 was about 50 million more than it was in 1980.
5. Write one additional fact about North America's population, based on the graph.
6. **Challenge:** Find the projected population for the next ten-year marker. Enter it on the graph.

B. Complete the graph below with population data about one North American country.

(name of country)

Name _____ Date _____

Cities of North America

This map of North America is labeled with letters that mark the locations of important cities. Match these letters with the correct names. Use the information provided below to help.

_____ 1. Chicago

_____ 2. Havana

_____ 3. Houston

_____ 4. Los Angeles

_____ 5. Managua

_____ 6. Mexico City

_____ 7. Montreal

_____ 8. New York City

_____ 9. Ottawa

_____ 10. Washington, D.C.

1. The third largest city in the United States, this city is located on the banks of Lake Michigan in the state of Illinois. It is famous as a transportation hub where rail, sea, and highways meet.

2. This is the capital and largest city of the island nation of Cuba. It is located on the western end of the island near the Gulf of Mexico.

3. The Gulf of Mexico is just off the coast where this city is located. It is the largest city in the state of Texas and is named after Sam Houston, a famous pioneer and leader.

4. Located on the west coast of the United States, this is the largest city west of the Rocky Mountains. It is famous for its climate, tourist attractions, and movie-making industry.

5. Located in Central America near a large lake that shares its name, this is the capital, largest city, and most important economic center of Nicaragua.

6. This city is one of the three largest in the world. It was built on the site of the ancient city of Tenochtitlan. Today it is the capital and most important economic center of Mexico.

7. This city has a very large French-speaking population. It is located on an island on the St. Lawrence River in Canada.

8. This city is the largest in the United States. It is the site of the headquarters of the United Nations and the financial district called Wall Street. The Statue of Liberty is located in its harbor.

9. This city got its name from a Native American word meaning *to trade*. It is now the capital city of Canada.

10. This city is located on the Potomac River in an area called the District of Columbia. It is the capital of the United States of America.

Name _____ Date _____

Languages of North America

Many languages are spoken in North America. However, many nations have adopted official languages or have commonly spoken languages. Identify the official or commonly spoken language or languages of each of the following countries.

Country   **Official Language(s)**

1. Antigua and Barbuda   _____

2. Bahamas   _____

3. Barbados   _____

4. Belize   _____

5. Canada   _____

6. Costa Rica   _____

7. Cuba   _____

8. Dominica   _____

9. Dominican Republic   _____

10. El Salvador   _____

11. Guatemala   _____

12. Haiti   _____

13. Honduras   _____

14. Jamaica   _____

15. Mexico   _____

16. Nicaragua   _____

17. Panama   _____

18. United States of America _____

19. a. List the countries whose official or commonly spoken language is Spanish.

_____

  b. Are these countries located in the northern or southern part of North America? _____

20. a. At one time, all of North America was controlled by European nations. People from these nations introduced changes to North America. How can you tell that the nations listed above were once controlled by European countries? _____

_____

  b. Which European countries controlled them? _____

_____

Religions of North America

(based on 1993 data)

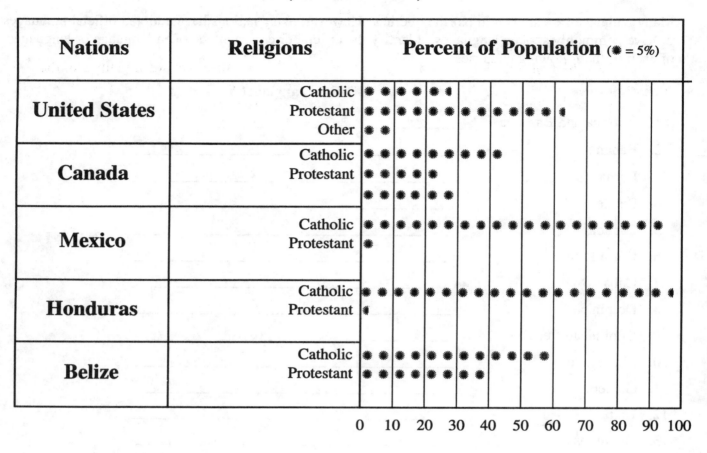

Nations	Religions	Percent of Population (✳ = 5%)
United States	Catholic	✳ ✳ ✳ ✳ ✳ ✳
	Protestant	✳ ✳ ✳ ✳ ✳ ✳ ✳ ✳ ✳ ✳ ✳ ✳
	Other	✳ ✳
Canada	Catholic	✳ ✳ ✳ ✳ ✳ ✳ ✳ ✳
	Protestant	✳ ✳ ✳ ✳ ✳
		✳ ✳ ✳ ✳ ✳ ✳
Mexico	Catholic	✳ ✳ ✳ ✳ ✳ ✳ ✳ ✳ ✳ ✳ ✳ ✳ ✳ ✳ ✳ ✳ ✳ ✳ ✳
	Protestant	✳
Honduras	Catholic	✳ ✳ ✳ ✳ ✳ ✳ ✳ ✳ ✳ ✳ ✳ ✳ ✳ ✳ ✳ ✳ ✳ ✳ ✳
	Protestant	✳
Belize	Catholic	✳ ✳ ✳ ✳ ✳ ✳ ✳ ✳ ✳
	Protestant	✳ ✳ ✳ ✳ ✳ ✳ ✳ ✳

0   10   20   30   40   50   60   70   80   90   100

Use the information on the graph and a map to complete the following.

1. What percentage of the population of Belize is Protestant?_____

2. Which country has the largest Protestant population? _____

3. What is the difference in the percentage of Mexico's and Canada's populations that follow

   Catholicism? _____

4. Guatemala is bordered by Mexico, Belize, and Honduras. Based on the information on the graph,

   what would you expect the most popular religion in Guatemala to be? _____

5. Write three additional facts about the information shown on the graph.

   a. _____

   b. _____

   c. _____

Name_____ Date _____

Traditional Clothing of
North America

Find photographs or illustrations or make sketches of the traditional costumes worn in three of the countries shown below. On the map, highlight the countries you have chosen. On the back of this page, write a description of each costume. Attach your pictures to this page.

North American Mountains

A mountain is a landform that stands much higher than its surroundings. It has steep slopes and sharp or rounded peaks. Mountains occur in the ocean as well as on land. Whether on land or under water, mountains are created over long periods of time by great forces in the earth.

Much of North America is mountainous. The largest mountain system in North America is the Rocky Mountains. It has more than a thousand peaks that are over 10,000 feet (300 meters) high. The Rocky Mountain range is often called the "Roof of North America." The sides of the mountains are filled with fossils of animals that once lived in the sea and rocks that were formed in the hot interior of the earth. Rich lodes of silver have been found in these mountains, not to mention a few nuggets of gold. Visitors to the Rockies enjoy their beautiful lakes, ski resorts, and wild game.

The Rockies stretch across the United States and Canada for more than 3,000 miles (4,800 km). In some areas, the mountains extend about 350 miles (563 km) wide. The provinces and states through which the Rocky Mountains stretch include Alaska, Washington, Montana, Idaho, Wyoming, Utah, Colorado, New Mexico, Alberta, British Columbia, and the Northwest and Yukon Territories.

To see just how large an area the Rocky Mountain range occupies in North America, follow the directions below to make a relief map. You may wish to work in a group for this activity.

Directions:

- Locate a North America relief map in an encyclopedia, atlas, or other reference book.
- Cut out an 18" x 24" (45 cm x 60 cm) piece of cardboard (covered with white paper) or white poster board.
- Make an outline of North America on the cardboard or poster board.
- Using modeling clay, form the mountain range across the area through which it extends. If possible, include the Appalachian Mountains on your map. Try to show the difference in the elevations and sizes of the two mountain ranges.
- Share your relief map with the class. Tell some interesting facts about this magnificent mountain range.

Applications to Other Sections of This Book:

Have the students make relief maps for other areas of the world. Use each for comparison.

North American Holidays

Holidays, feasts, and festivals are celebrated throughout North America. Some, such as Easter and Christmas, are observed throughout the continent but with different traditions and customs. Others, such as Cinco de Mayo (Mexico), Independence Day (United States), and Victoria Day (Canada), are unique to one area or people.

To make a diorama featuring one North American holiday, follow the directions below.

Materials:

- medium to large cardboard box
- pencil, pen, word processor, or typewriter
- colored pencils, paints, crayons, or markers
- research materials
- scissors
- glue or tape
- colored paper
- white tagboard

Directions:

- Choose and research a holiday.
- Construct a diorama that depicts an important ritual or tradition of the holiday. For free-standing elements, copy or trace figures onto white paper. Color them appropriately and then glue them to tagboard. After the glue has dried, cut out the figures, making sure to leave a tab at the bottom to allow you to glue the figure to the base of your diorama.
- On the top or front of your diorama, attach a short report in which you identify and describe the holiday, feast, or festival in general and the scene you have created in particular.

Applications to Other Sections of This Book:

Holidays are celebrated throughout the world. An interesting way to study world cultures is through their holidays. Use this or other holiday-based activities to investigate other areas of the world.

Boundary Map of South America

Physical Map of South America

Physical Geography of South America

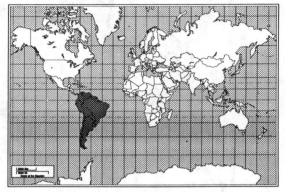

Location: South America is located south of North America and north of Antarctica. It is bordered by the Pacific Ocean to the west, the Caribbean Sea to the north and the Atlantic Ocean to the east. All of South America is located in the western hemisphere. About 20% of the continent lies above the equator in the northern hemisphere. The remaining 80% is in the southern hemisphere.

Area: South America is the fourth continent in area with approximately 6,900,000 square miles (17,800,000 km²) of land. It is, therefore, about twice the area of the United States. The greatest distance from north to south is 4,750 miles (7,645 km). The greatest distance from east to west is 3,200 miles (5,150 km). The highest point on the continent is the summit of Mount Aconcagua, 22,831 feet (6,959 m). The lowest point is on Valdes Peninsula 131 feet (40 m) below sea level.

Climate: For the most part, South America is warm to hot around the year. The high Andes is the only area that is cold all year. In the part of the continent that is south of the equator, January is a warmer month than July. In lands of the southern hemisphere, winter is in July and August and summer in January and February.

Precipitation in most of South America is medium to heavy. Medium precipitation is 40 to 80 inches (100 to 200 cm) per year, and heavy is more than 80 inches (200 cm). One area in the northern part of the continent receives more than 350 inches (890 cm) of rain each year. The other extreme is in the Atacama Desert where less than one-half inch (1.25 cm) of rain falls in a typical year.

Landforms: South America has many dramatic and impressive physical features. Among them are deserts, mountains, rivers, rain forests, and waterfalls.

Along the narrow band of western lowlands and in the southeast region are two very dry areas, the Atacama Desert and Patagonia. These are interesting regions partly because their dryness is caused by the Andes even though they are on opposite sides of these mountains. In the part of South America where the Atacama is located, rain clouds come from the east and are intercepted by the Andes. Just south of the Atacama, rain clouds come from the west and are intercepted by the Andes before they can deposit any rain on Patagonia.

Running along the spine of South America are the Andes Mountains, the longest continuous mountain range on land. All ten of the western hemisphere's tallest mountains are located in this range, including Aconcagua, the highest peak.

The longest and most famous river in South America is the Amazon. With its tributaries, this river drains a huge amount of the continent. It is valuable as a transportation route and as the site of the world's largest rain forest.

Many spectacular waterfalls are located throughout South America. The waterfall with the greatest drop in the world, Angel Falls, is located in northern South America.

Name _____ Date _____

Physical Features of South America

Some major features of South America are labeled with letters on the map. Match the letters to the names of the features listed below.

_____ 1. Amazon River

_____ 2. Andes Mountains

_____ 3. Atacama Desert

_____ 4. Brazilian Highlands

_____ 5. Cape Horn

_____ 6. Falkland Islands

_____ 7. Galapagos Islands

_____ 8. Gran Chaco

_____ 9. Guiana Highlands

_____ 10. Gulf of Guayaquil

_____ 11. Gulf of San Jorge

_____ 12. Mato Grosso Plateau

_____ 13. Lake Titicaca

_____ 14. Paraguay River

_____ 15. Tierra del Fuego

Name _____ Date _____

Rivers of South America

Use the clues to help you match the letters on the map to the correct names.

_____ 1. **Amazon River**—This river's source is in the Andes. It flows eastward 4,000 miles (6,400 km) to its mouth at the Atlantic Ocean. It is the longest river in South America and the second longest in the world.

_____ 2. **Iguacu River**—This river flows westward from the Great Escarpment in southeast Brazil until it reaches the Parana River. It is famous for Iguaco Falls.

_____ 3. **Madeira River**—The Madeira begins near the border between Brazil and Bolivia. It flows northeast 2,000 miles (3,200 km) through the Amazon Basin until it joins the Amazon River.

_____ 4. **Orinoco River**—This river's sources are located near the border between Venezuela and Brazil. During its 1,300 mile (2,080 km) journey it flows northwest, north, and east before reaching the Atlantic Ocean.

_____ 5. **Paraguay River**—Beginning in Brazil, this river flows southward 1,584 miles (2,534.4 km) through Brazil, Paraguay, and between Paraguay and Argentina. It empties into the Parana River.

_____ 6. **Parana River**—This is the second longest river in South America. Its source is in southern Brazil, and its mouth is at the Rio de la Plata. It is fed by the Paraguay and Iguacu Rivers.

_____ 7. **Colorado River**—This river is in the far south and begins in the Andes. On its eastward journey to the Atlantic Ocean it passes between the Patagonia and Pampas regions of Argentina.

_____ 8. **Purus River**—This is the third longest river in South America. Its source is in the Andes Mountains within Peru. It flows northwest of the Madeira River and empties into the Amazon.

_____ 9. **Rio Sáo Francisco**—Flowing northeast from its source in eastern Brazil, this river bends to the southeast as it approaches its mouth in the Atlantic. It is famous for Paulo Afonso Falls.

_____ 10. **Uruguay River**—Before it empties into the Rio de la Plata, this river flows 1,000 miles (1,600 km) from its source in southeast Brazil. It begins by flowing westward but gradually bends to the south.

Name_____ Date _____

Mountains of South America

A. Complete the table, using the mountains named in the word bank. Use reference books to find their heights. Then, list them in order by height.

Aconcagua	Bonete	Cachi	Huascaran	Llullaillaco
El Libertador	Mercedario	Ojos del Salado	Pissis	Tupungato

	Name	Country	Height
1.			
2.			
3.			
4.			
5.			
6.			
7.			
8.			
9.			
10.			

B. Make a vertical bar graph to compare the five tallest mountains.

(mountain names)

Bodies of Water in South America

Cut out the bodies of water. Glue them in their proper places on the map provided.

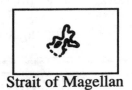
Strait of Magellan

Lake Titicaca

Gulf of San Matias

Lake Poopo

Rio de la Plata

Mouths of the Amazon River

Gulf of San Jorge

Gulf of Guayaquil

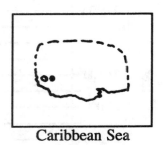
Caribbean Sea

Bodies of Water in
South America *(cont.)*

Glue the cutouts from the previous page onto the map in their correct locations.

Name _____   Date _____

Deserts of South America

Describe how the following are related to South America deserts. Color the desert areas yellow on the map.

1. Atacama _____

   _____

2. Andes Mountains _____

   _____

3. copper _____

   _____

4. Loa River _____

   _____

   _____

5. Patagonia _____

   _____

   _____

6. Sechura _____

   _____

   _____

7. sheep _____

   _____

   _____

8. sodium nitrate _____

   _____

   _____

Name _____ Date _____

Islands of South America

Use an atlas to match the latitudes and longitudes of the islands with their names.

76 W
┼── 49 S

1. _____

75 W
┼── 45 S

2. _____

59 W
┼── 51 S

3. _____

78 W
┼── 32 S

4. _____

64 W
┼── 11 N

5. _____

74 W
┼── 42 S

6. _____

69 W
┼── 12 N

7. _____

37 W
┼── 55 S

8. _____

62 W
┼── 12 N

9. _____

68 W
┼── 54 S

10. _____

61 W
┼── 10 N

11. _____

90 W
┼── 0

12. _____

A. Chiloé

B. Chonos

C. Curaçao

D. Falklands

E. Galapagos Archipelago

F. Grenada

G. Margarita

H. Robinson Crusoe

I. South Georgia

J. Tierra del Fuego

K. Trinidad

L. Wellington

Name _____ Date _____

Climate of South America

Average Yearly Precipitation

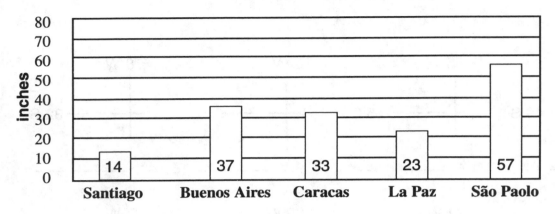

Average January and July Temperatures

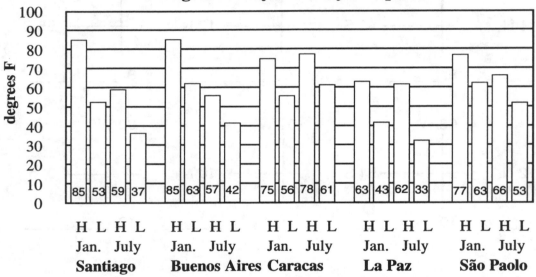

Growing Seasons

Santiago	Buenos Aires	Caracas	La Paz	São Paolo
8 to 10 months	10 to 12 months	12 months	6 to 8 months	10 to 12 months

Use the data to determine if the statements are true or false. Rewrite the false statements to make them correct.

_____ 1. São Paolo and Caracas experience the greatest average precipitation.

_____ 2. Santiago experiences the greatest difference between January and July high temperatures.

_____ 3. The difference between the January and July low temperatures in La Paz is about 10 degrees.

_____ 4. São Paolo and Buenos Aires have the same growing season because their average precipitation is similar.

_____ 5. Only people in Caracas are able to grow crops outdoors in winter.

Name _____ Date _____

Products and Resources of South America

Use an encyclopedia and/or atlas to find the information needed to complete the chart. One is given as an example. (Note: Use *agriculture, manufacturing, mining, forestry,* or *fishing* for "Type of Product.")

Product	Leading South American Producer	Type of Product	World Rank
bananas	Brazil	agriculture	1
bauxite			
cattle			
coffee			
copper			
fish			
forest products			
gold			
iron ore			
lead			
manganese			
sugar cane			
tin			
wool			

Use information on the chart to answer the questions.

1. How many different countries are listed on your chart? _____

2. Which country is most often listed? _____

3. What type of product is most often listed? _____

4. Which country listed seems to be the wealthiest? _____

    Why? _____

    _____

5. How might the size of a country be a factor in the amount of products and resources it produces?

    _____

Nam _____   Date _____

Vegetation of South America

Write one fact about the vegetation that grows in the areas listed below. Lightly shade the correct areas with the colors indicated. Use reference books such as atlases and encyclopedias as sources for this information.

1. Deserts (yellow)

   _____

   _____

2. Grasslands (steppes, savannas, Mediterranean) (yellow-green)

   _____

   _____

3. Forests (tropical rain, needleleaf, broadleaf, mixed) (green)

   _____

   _____

4. Tundra (blue-green)

   _____

   _____

5. Ice and snow (white)

   _____

   _____

Animals of South America

The animals listed below are found in South America. In the first column, identify the animal as a *mammal, reptile, bird,* or *fish*. In the second column, write "endangered" if the animal is on the endangered species list. Match five of the names with the correct pictures.

1. toucan   _____ _____

2. llama   _____ _____

3. alpaca   _____ _____

4. vicuna   _____ _____

5. marmoset   _____ _____

6. jaguar   _____ _____

7. vampire bat   _____ _____

8. Galapagos tortoise _____ _____

9. giant anteater _____ _____

10. rhea   _____ _____

11. Andean condor _____ _____

12. capuchin   _____ _____

13. capybara   _____ _____

14. guanaco   _____ _____

15. anaconda   _____ _____

Human Geography of South America

Population: As of 1990, about 287 million people live in South America. Of these, more than half live in the country of Brazil. South America is part of the region known as Latin America, which also includes the Caribbean Islands, Mexico, and Central America. Most of the people of this region are descendants of European, American Indian, African, or mixed ancestry.

Lifestyles: About 75% (215 million) of South America's population lives in urban areas. The larger cities are similar in appearance to cities in the United States, with highrise office buildings, apartments, and single-family homes. In older sections of cities, the houses were built in the Spanish style, using adobe, stone, and wood. Large slum areas usually border South American cities.

The people of rural South America are usually poorer than those living in cities. They live in small wood or mud-brick houses, usually lacking electricity and indoor plumbing. Few own their own land, having instead to work on the large farms and ranches of wealthy landowners.

Clothing in South America varies with the region and ethnic group. Many people living in urban areas wear clothing like that worn in cities of the United States. Traditional clothing includes hats, loose-fitting cotton shirts and pants, and sandals for men and long skirts, loose-fitting blouses, and shawls for women. Ponchos are popular with both men and women. Wheat, potatoes, fish, cassava, and fruits are common in the diets of South Americans. Meat is generally too expensive for most South Americans, although people of the far south eat more beef because many cattle are raised in this area. Foods are often seasoned with onions and peppers.

Languages: Most of the people of South America speak either Spanish or Portuguese. About two-thirds speak Spanish and most of the one-third who speak Portuguese live in Brazil. Traditional languages are still spoken by many Native Americans. A smaller number of South Americans speak English or Dutch as their principal language.

Education: South American governments have been working very hard to provide education to all of their people. Over the past few decades, many more children have been given the opportunity to receive at least an elementary education. More and more South Americans are continuing on to high school and college. Still, in many rural areas and city slums, children are unable to attend school because there are not enough available schools or because they are needed to help make money for their families.

Religious Beliefs: A great majority of South Americans are Christians. Of these, most are Roman Catholics, while a growing percentage of the population is joining Protestant faiths. Some South Americans are Jewish, Hindu, or Moslem, especially in the north.

Name _____   Date _____

Population of South America

A. Complete the graph, using the information provided.

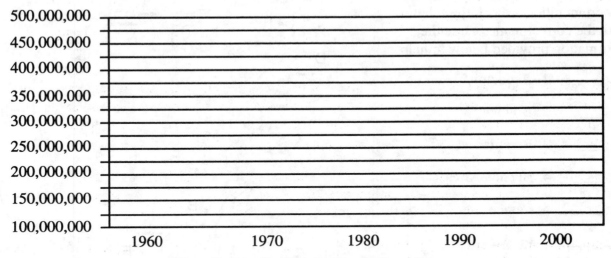

Population Growth in South America
(rounded to nearest 5 million)

1. In 1960, South America's population was about 145 million.
2. By 1970, the population had increased by about 45 million.
3. In 1980, the population was about 40 million more than 200 million.
4. South America's population in 1990 was about 60 million more than it was in 1980.
5. Write one additional fact about South America's population, based on the graph.
6. **Challenge:** Find the projected population for the next ten-year marker. Enter it on the graph.

B. Complete the graph below with population data about one South American country.

(name of country)

Cities of South America

This map of South America is labeled with letters that mark the locations of important cities. Match these letters with the correct names. Use the information provided below to help.

_____ 1. Asunción

_____ 2. Bogota

_____ 3. Brasilia

_____ 4. Buenos Aires

_____ 5. Caracas

_____ 6. La Paz

_____ 7. Lima

_____ 8. Montevideo

_____ 9. Quito

_____10. Rio de Janeiro

_____11. Santiago

_____12. São Paulo

_____13. Sucre

1. This city is the capital, largest city, and chief port of Paraguay.
2. This city is the capital and largest city of Colombia.
3. Located about 600 miles (960 km) from Rio de Janeiro is this city, the capital of Brazil.
4. This city is the capital, largest city, and chief port of Argentina.
5. This city is the capital and largest city of Venezuela.
6. This is the largest city of Bolivia. It is about 12,000 feet (3,600 m) above sea level.
7. This city is the capital and largest city of Peru.
8. This city is the capital, largest city, and chief port of Uruguay.
9. This capital of Ecuador is located in the Andes Mountains.
10. Famous for the annual carnival, this is the second largest city of Brazil.
11. This city is the capital and largest city of Chile.
12. This is the largest city in Brazil and South America.
13. This is the official capital of Bolivia.

Name _____ Date _____

Languages of South America

Many languages are spoken in South America. However, many nations have adopted official languages or have commonly spoken languages. Identify the official or commonly spoken language or languages of each of the following countries.

Country	**Official Language(s)**
1. Argentina	_____
2. Bolivia	_____
3. Brazil	_____
4. Chile	_____
5. Colombia	_____
6. Ecuador	_____
7. Guyana	_____
8. Paraguay	_____
9. Peru	_____
10. Suriname	_____
11. Uruguay	_____
12. Venezuela	_____

The following are territories without their own governments. On the first line, identify the principal language(s) spoken. On the second line, identify the country that controls the territory.

13. Falkland Islands

_____

_____

14. French Guiana

_____

_____

15. a. Which language is spoken in most nations of South America? _____

    b. In which area(s) of South America are these countries located? _____

16. a. At one time, all South America was controlled by European nations. People from these nations introduced changes to South America. How can you tell that the nations listed above were once controlled by European countries? _____

    b. Which European countries controlled them? _____

_____

Name _____ Date _____

Religions of South America

(based on 1993 data)

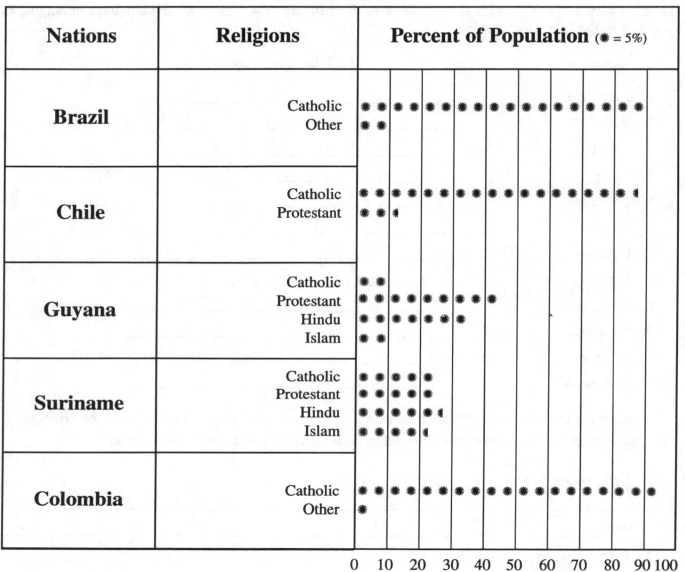

Nations	Religions	Percent of Population (✴ = 5%)
Brazil	Catholic Other	✴ ✴ ✴ ✴ ✴ ✴ ✴ ✴ ✴ ✴ ✴ ✴ ✴ ✴ ✴ ✴ ✴ ✴ ✴ ✴
Chile	Catholic Protestant	✴ ✴ ✴ ✴ ✴ ✴ ✴ ✴ ✴ ✴ ✴ ✴ ✴ ✴ ✴ ✴ ✴ ◀ ✴ ✴ ◀
Guyana	Catholic Protestant Hindu Islam	✴ ✴ ✴ ✴ ✴ ✴ ✴ ✴ ✴ ✴ ✴ ✴ ✴ ✴ ✴ ✴ ✴ ✴ ✴
Suriname	Catholic Protestant Hindu Islam	✴ ✴ ✴ ✴ ✴ ✴ ✴ ✴ ✴ ✴ ✴ ✴ ✴ ✴ ✴ ◀ ✴ ✴ ✴ ✴ ◀
Colombia	Catholic Other	✴ ✴ ✴ ✴ ✴ ✴ ✴ ✴ ✴ ✴ ✴ ✴ ✴ ✴ ✴ ✴ ✴ ✴ ✴

```
0   10   20   30   40   50   60   70   80   90 100
```

Use the information on the graph and a map to complete the following.

1. What percentage of the population of Guyana is Muslim? _____

2. Which country has the largest Catholic population? _____

3. What is the difference in percentage between Chile's and Suriname's populations that are

   Protestants? _____

4. What religion is probably most popular in the nations not listed? _____

Name_____ Date _____

Traditional Clothing of South America

Find photographs or illustrations or make sketches of the traditional costumes worn in three of the countries shown below. On the map, highlight the countries you have chosen. On the back of this page, write a description of each costume. Attach your pictures to this page.

South American Biomes

According to *The World Book Encyclopedia*, a biome is "a plant and animal community that covers a large geographical area. The boundaries of different biomes on land are determined mainly by climate." The major land biomes are the tundra, taiga, coniferous forest, deciduous forest, chaparral, desert, grassland, savanna, tropical rain forest, and highlands.

The major biomes of South America are the deciduous forest, chaparral, desert, grassland, tropical rain forest, and highlands. The deciduous forests of South America are located in the Guiana and Brazilian Highlands. Areas of chaparral are found in the far south of Brazil and central Chile. One large desert biome is between the Pacific Ocean and the Andes Mountains from northern Peru to central Chile. The other desert biome is called Patagonia in southern Argentina. The great grassland biome of South America is called the pampas and is located in northern Argentina. Probably the most famous biome of South America is the tropical rain forest. Most of the Amazon River Basin and northeast and northwest coastal areas are covered by tropical rain forests. The highland biome is the Andes Mountains.

To make a biome mural, follow the directions given below.

Materials:

- reference materials
- butcher paper
- pencils, crayons, paints, markers, and/or pastels
- writing paper
- pen, typewriter, and/or word processor
- glue or transparent tape

Directions:

- Choose a South American biome. Using reference materials, locate and identify at least five important plants and animals that live in your biome and find pictures of the terrain.
- On a sheet of butcher paper, make a mural of your biome, showing the plants, animals, and terrain you have identified.
- Label the plants, animals, and other characteristics of your biome and write a description of each to display with your mural.

Carnival Time

Carnival in Brazil is a national time of celebration and merrymaking. It lasts for four days and five nights, beginning at 11 P.M. on the Friday before Ash Wednesday. Ash Wednesday is the first day of Lent, an important religious season in the Christian religion. Christians are expected to observe the forty days of Lent with fasting, prayer, and self-sacrifice.

Carnival, like Mardi Gras in the United States, is world famous. It attracts people from all over the world who come to watch or join in parties, parades, or other entertainments. Except for street vendors, businesses close for the four days. The vendors sell food, drink, and souvenirs.

One important part of Carnival is the contest among samba "schools." These schools are large groups of people from poor neighborhoods who prepare dances, skits, music, floats, and costumes for presenting at Carnival. Forming percussion bands, called *bateria,* is a popular part of a samba school. The twelve finalist schools join in colorful parades before the top prize is awarded. The middle and upper classes join the parade's spectators, but they also give and attend parties. Upper-class parties are often costume balls in which participants wear costumes of legendary or fairy tale characters.

To stage a class Carnival, complete with costumes, dancing, food, skits, music, and songs, divide the class into samba schools to compete with one another. If two or more classes participate, each class can be its own samba school. Invite other classes and/or your parents to your Carnival.

To hold a Carnival, you will need to do or prepare the following things:

- **Costumes:** Create costumes that reflect South American history or culture.
- **Skits:** Enact scenes from South American history or literature. Perform them as a readers' theater or with full staging.
- **Dancing:** Learn the samba or other dances popular in South America.
- **Food:** Research to find authentic South American dishes. Foods popular in Brazil include manjioco (a kind of potato), macaroni, rice, olives, greens, beans, bananas, pineapples, mangos, oranges, carrots, lettuce, seafood, beef, poultry, corn, and pork.
- **Music:** Find and learn traditional and popular songs of Brazil and South America. Create a *bateria.*

Boundary Map of Antarctica

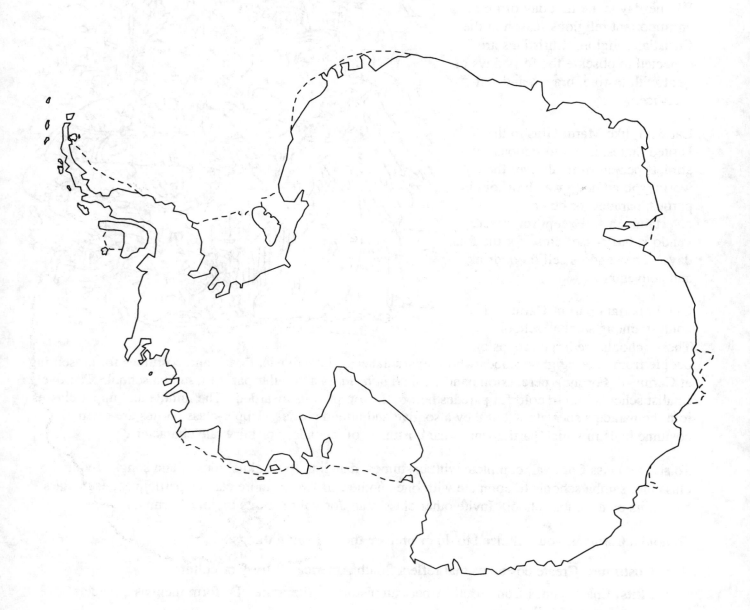

Physical Map of Antarctica

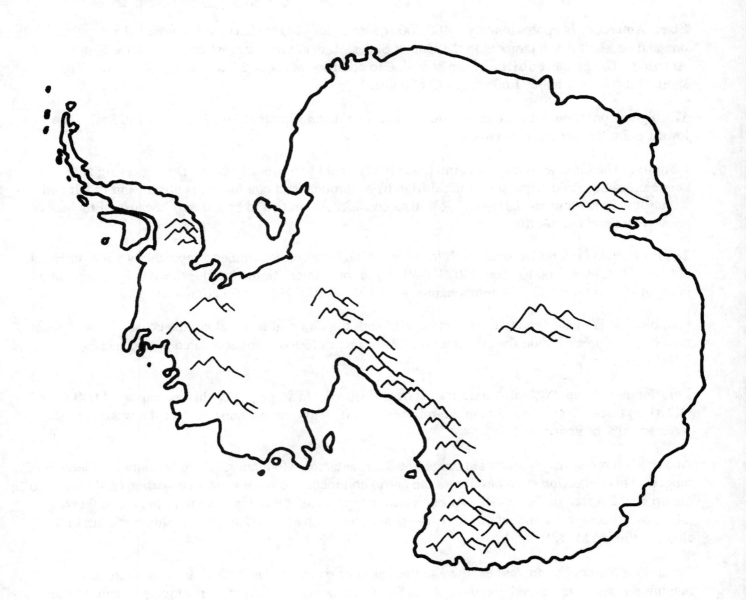

Physical Geography of Antarctica

Location: Antarctica is located in the southern hemisphere almost entirely within the Arctic Circle. It surrounds the South Pole, the southernmost place on Earth. It is bordered by the Pacific Ocean, the Indian Ocean, and the Atlantic Ocean.

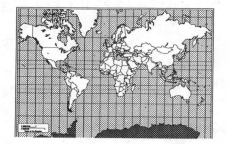

Size: Antarctica is approximately 5,400,000 square miles (14,000,000 km²) in area, which makes it one and one-half times larger than the United States. It is the fifth largest continent after South America. The greatest distance from coastline to coastline is about 2,800 miles (4,400 km). The shortest distance is about 1,600 miles (2,600 km).

The highest point on the continent is the summit of Vinson Massif at 16,864 feet (5,140 km). The lowest point has yet to be discovered.

Climate: The climate throughout Antarctica is very cold to extremely cold. During spring and summer months (mid-September to mid-March) Antarctica is in continuous sunlight, and in fall and winter it is in continuous darkness. Scientists consider Antarctica to be a desert because of its lack of native plant and animal life.

Temperature in Antarctica varies with location. Along the coast, summer temperatures climb to about 30° F (-1° C) but drop to about -40° F (-40° C) in the winter. In the interior the average temperature is about -57° F (-150° C), but temperatures at or below -100° F (-73° C) are not unusual.

Precipitation is mostly snow in Antarctica, although fog and rain occur along the coast. Coastal areas receive more precipitation than the interior, 12–24 inches (30–60 cm) compared to 4–6 inches (10–15 cm).

Landforms: About 98% of Antarctica is covered by ice. In some places this ice cap is 14,000 feet (4,270 m) thick. That is more than 2.5 miles (4.8 km). This cap contains 70% of the world's fresh water or 90% of its ice.

Antarctica has one major mountain range, the Transantarctic Mountains, which is really a collection of ranges. This collection stretches across the entire continent, from the western coastline of Ross Sea to the tip of the Antarctic Peninsula. At one point it appears as if there is a break in the range; however, this is only because the mountains in this area are covered by ice and snow. The highest peak in the chain is Vinson Massif.

Because of the cold temperatures, there are no lakes or rivers on Antarctica. Instead, there are huge, moving masses of ice called *glaciers*. Actually, all of the ice of Antarctica is moving toward the sea. It is constantly being forced outward by its own weight. Antarctic glaciers, however, move faster than the rest of the ice.

A permanent ice formation that extends out over the sea is called an *ice shelf*. Several massive ice shelves have formed in the coastal areas of Antarctica. For example, much of Ross Sea and Weddell Sea are covered by ice shelves.

Physical Features of Antarctica

Some major features of Antarctica are labeled with letters on the map. Match the letters to the names of the features listed below.

_____ 1. Amundsen Sea

_____ 2. Alexander Island

_____ 3. Antarctic Peninsula

_____ 4. Bellingshausen Sea

_____ 5. Filchner Ice Shelf

_____ 6. Lambert Glacier

_____ 7. McMurdo Sound

_____ 8. Ronne Ice Shelf

_____ 9. Ross Ice Shelf

_____ 10. South Pole

_____ 11. Weddell Sea

_____ 12. Transantarctic Mountains

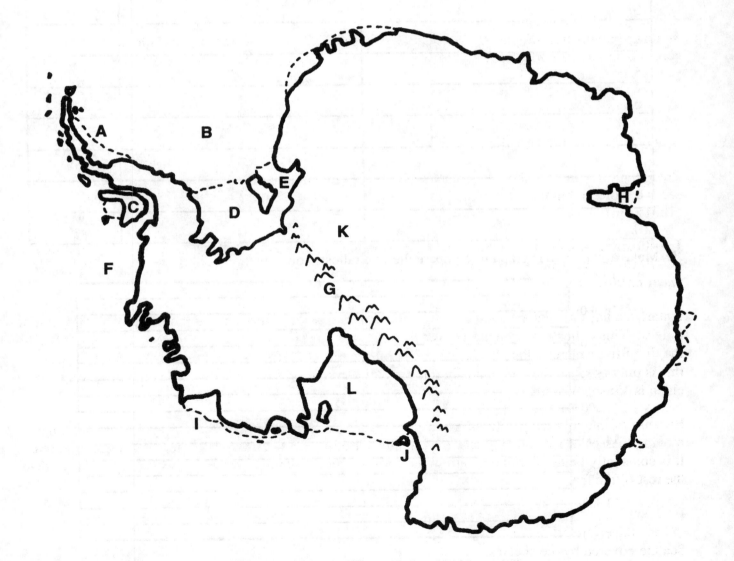

Mountains of Antarctica

A. Complete the table, using the mountains named in the word bank. List them in order by height.

| Bell | Elizabeth | Epperly | Gardner | Kirkpatrick |
| Mackellar | Markham | Shinn | Tyree | Vinson Massif |

	Name	Country	Height
1.			
2.			
3.			
4.			
5.			
6.			
7.			
8.			
9.			
10.			

B. Make a vertical bar graph to compare the five tallest mountains.

(mountain names)

Seas and Ice Shelves of Antarctica

Cut out the seas and ice shelves. Glue them in their proper places on the map provided on the next page. (Note: It may be necessary to glue an ice shelf over a sea.)

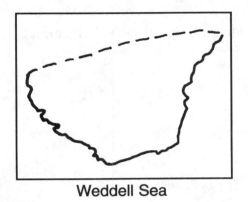

Weddell Sea

Amundsen Sea

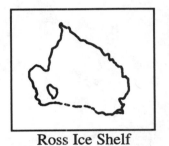

Ross Ice Shelf

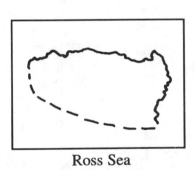

Ross Sea

Filchner Ice Shelf

Ronne Ice Shelf

Bellingshausen Sea

Riiser-Larsen
Ice Shelf

Amery Ice Shelf

Seas and Ice Shelves
of Antarctica *(cont.)*

Glue the cutouts of seas and ice shelves from the previous page onto the map below in their correct locations.

Name _____ Date _____

Lands and Islands of Antarctica

Coastal regions of Antarctica have been named after explorers, rulers, and other individuals. Some of these areas have been labeled with letters on the map below. Match the letters with the correct names.

_____1. Coats Land

_____2. Ellsworth Land

_____3. Mac-Robertson Land

_____4. Marie Byrd Land

_____5. Palmer Land

_____6. Queen Maud Land

_____7. Victoria Land

_____8. Wilkes Land

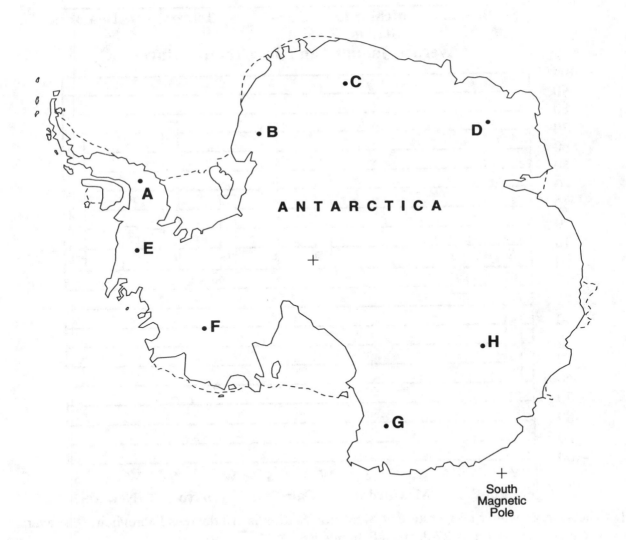

Name_____ Date _____

Climate of Antarctica

Complete the graphs, using the information provided below.

Average Yearly Precipitation

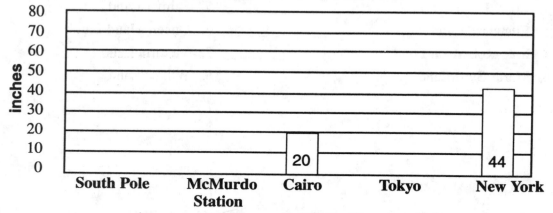

Average January and July Temperatures

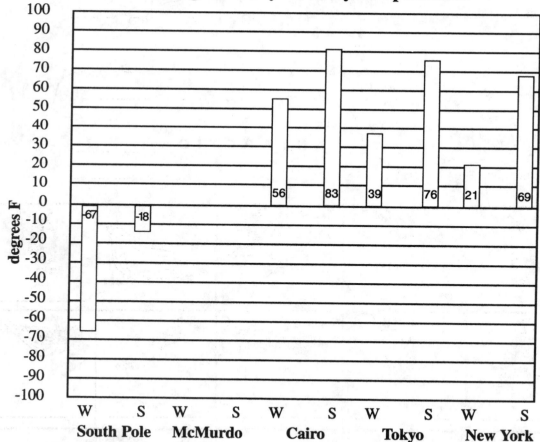

1. The average winter temperature at McMurdo Station is -18 degrees Fahrenheit. The average summer temperature is 27 degrees Fahrenheit.

2. The average amount of precipitation that falls in Tokyo, Japan, each year is 62 inches.

3. The average amount of precipitation that falls at the South Pole is about 2 inches.

4. About 24 inches of snow falls at McMurdo Station each year.

Name _____ Date _____

Animals of Antarctica

The animals listed below live at least part of each year on and/or around Antarctica. In the first column, identify the animal as a *mammal, reptile,* or *bird*. In the second column, write "endangered" if the animal is on the endangered species list. Match five of the names with the correct pictures.

1. Adelie penguin   _____   _____

2. Arctic tern   _____   _____

3. blue whale   _____   _____

4. Cape pigeon   _____   _____

5. elephant seal   _____   _____

6. emperor penguin   _____   _____

7. fulmar   _____   _____

8. humpback whale   _____   _____

9. leopard seal   _____   _____

10. orca   _____   _____

11. petrel   _____   _____

12. Ross seal   _____   _____

13. skua   _____   _____

14. sperm whale   _____   _____

15. Rockhopper penguin   _____   _____

A Land of Glaciers

Millions of years ago, before it became the ice-capped continent it is today, Antarctica was an ice-free part of a huge mass of land. This mass also included the lands that are now Africa, Australia, India, and South America. As this land mass broke apart and Antarctica drifted southward, glaciers began to form. Glaciers are huge masses of slow-moving ice.

Along Antarctica's rugged coast are glacier-filled valleys. These gigantic glaciers move slowly downhill toward the sea, carrying with them soil and rocks that they scrape from the mountain slopes and valley floors. At the front edge of the glaciers, chunks of ice break off and fall into the sea, forming icebergs that float in the oceans surrounding the continent.

To better understand the effects of glaciers, try this experiment.

What will happen?

Materials:

- small milk carton
- rocks
- sand
- water
- dirt
- freezer
- tape

Directions:

- Fill the carton 1/4 full with sand and rocks. Fill the rest with water. Tape it closed, shake it, and freeze it.
- Outside, make a mound of the dirt.
- When frozen, peel off the carton and place the ice block on top of the dirt mound. Draw a picture (before).
- Watch what happens. Draw a picture (after).
- Compare the pictures and discuss the results. Can a glacier really dig a valley as it moves?

Applications to Other Sections of This Book:

Glaciers are also found on the continents of North America, Europe, Asia, and South America. Incorporating this glacier activity into the study of these continents would, therefore, be appropriate.

Race to the Pole

At the beginning of the 1900s, explorers from the world over began to explore and map the North and South Poles. Over time, this exploration became a race to see who would become the first to reach each of the Poles. The North Pole was reached for the first time in 1909. A race for the South Pole began in 1911 between two parties, one English and the other Norwegian. The Norwegian party, led by Roald Amundsen, reached the South Pole five weeks before the English, led by Robert Scott. The Norwegians returned safely to their base. All five English explorers died on their return journey.

Your class can hold its own "race to the Pole" by following this activity. First, find out more about Antarctic explorers and their experiences by reading books and other resources from your school or local library or by viewing videos about Antarctica. Then, use the materials and directions below to hold your own race to the South Pole.

Materials:

- tokens
- die
- index cards
- transparency film or large sheet of paper

Directions:

- Enlarge the map (gameboard) on this page by transferring it to transparency film and projecting it onto a large sheet of paper for copying, or lay the transparency on an overhead projector and use the projection as your gameboard.

- Assign tokens to individuals or teams.

- Have each team or individual find facts about Antarctica. Make questions for each fact and write each question and answer on an index card.

- To play the game, each team/player asks the team/player to the left a question from their cards. The other team/player must answer the question correctly to roll the die and move. Fact cards may be consulted for the answers. If no answer or an incorrect answer is given, the token may not be moved.

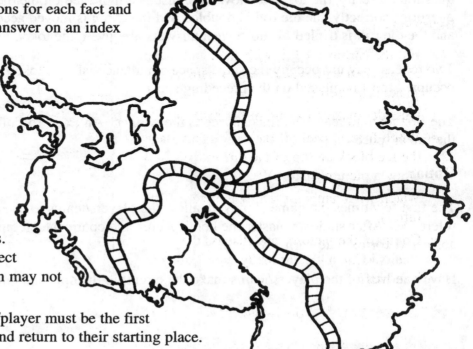

- To win the game, a team/player must be the first to reach the South Pole and return to their starting place.

World Geography Game

The World Geography Game is a board game played by two to six individuals or teams. It is designed to test your students' knowledge of basic facts about world geography. The object of the game is to be the first individual or team to complete a circuit around the world. This is done by combining luck (rolls of the die) with skill (the ability to correctly answer questions about the world).

Equipment

- **Game Board**—The game board (pages 153–156) consists of a circuit rail of 66 spaces printed on a map of the world. You will need to provide a die and tokens for each player/team. Attach each quarter-section of the map together to make a complete game board. Glue the game board to tagboard, color it, and laminate it, if possible.

- **Question and Answer Sheets**—The question and answer sheets are used by the teacher/ moderator as a source for questions and answers for the game. There is a set of three questions for each space on the game board.

Rules

All players/teams begin with a token on the start/finish space. It is necessary for one person to remain neutral and serve as the moderator. Roll the die to determine which player/team will go first.

The first turn is the only one during which a player/team is not required to answer a question. The player/team rolls the die and moves the indicated number of spaces on the map. Before the second and each successive turn, each player/team is asked three questions about the space occupied by the token. The teacher/moderator asks the questions drawn from the question and answer sheet. The questions and answers correspond to the numbered spaces on the gameboard. If a player/team answers one question correctly, the token is moved the distance indicated on the die. If the player/team answers two questions correctly, the die roll is doubled and the token is moved accordingly. Three correct responses and the die roll is tripled. If no correct answers are given, the token may not be moved.

Two tokens may not occupy the same space simultaneously. A token moved to a space already occupied must be placed on the preceding space.

The first team to reach the finish space is the winner. An exact roll of the die is not required to enter the finish space.

Options

The first few times the game is played, allow the players/teams to use atlases and/or textbooks for reference. After students master the hemispheres and continents, require that all three questions be answered correctly to earn a die roll.

Have one-half of the players/teams make the circuit in the opposite direction of the other half.

World Geography Game Board

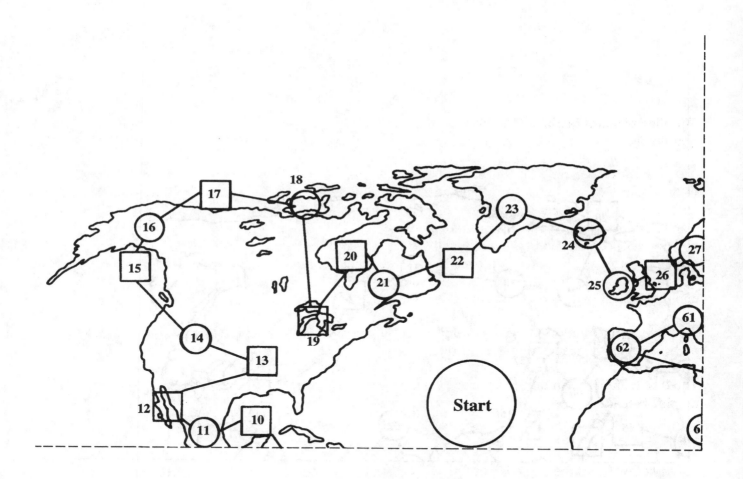

World Geography Game Board (cont.)

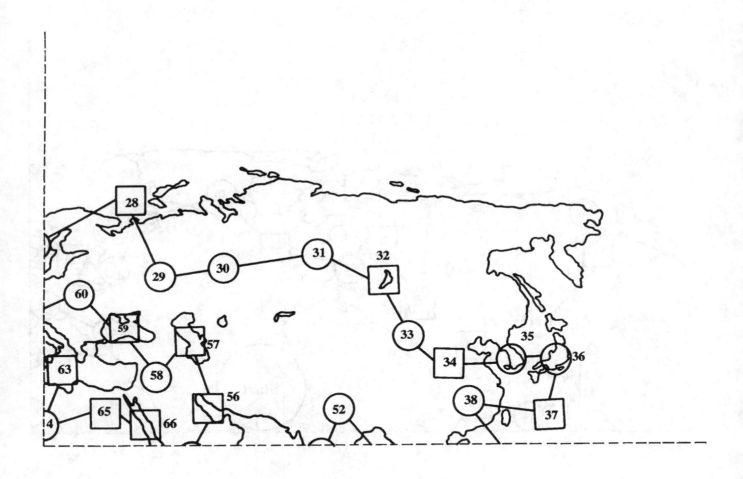

154

World Geography Game Board *(cont.)*

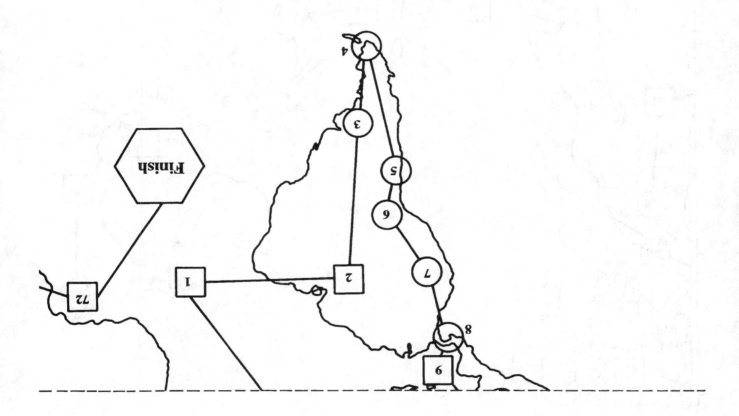

World Geography Game Board *(cont.)*

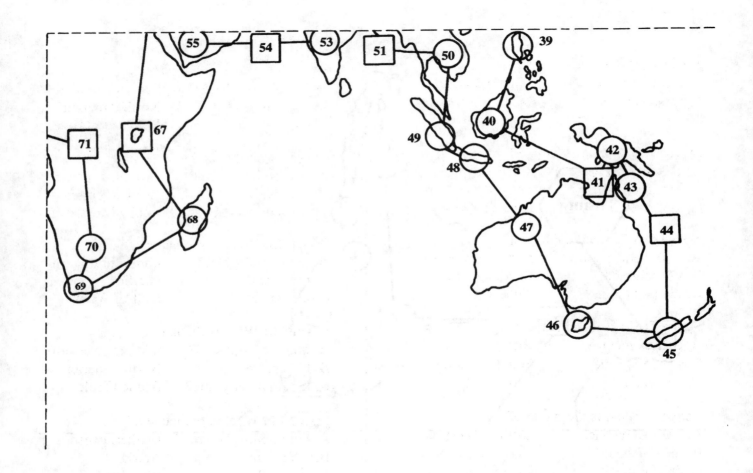

World Geography Game Question/Answer Sheet

Space 1: What is the name of . . .
A. both hemispheres?   southern/western
B. the ocean?   Atlantic
C. the imaginary line?   equator

Space 2: What is the name of . . .
A. both hemispheres?   southern/western
B. the continent?   South America
C. the river basin?   Amazon Basin

Space 3: What is the name of . . .
A. both hemispheres?   southern/western
B. the continent?   South America
C. the grassy plain?   pampas

Space 4: What is the name of . . .
A. both hemispheres?   southern/western
B. the continent?   South America
C. the cape   Cape Horn

Space 5: What is the name of . . .
A. both hemispheres?   southern/western
B. the continent?   South America
C. the desert?   Atacama Desert

Space 6: What is the name of . . .
A. both hemispheres?   southern/western
B. the continent?   South America
C. the mountains?   Andes

Space 7: What is the name of . . .
A. both hemispheres?   southern/western
B. the continent?   South America
C. the country?   Peru

Space 8: What is the name of . . .
A. both hemispheres?   northern/western
B. the continent?   North America
C. the isthmus?   Panama

Space 9: What is the name of . . .
A. both hemispheres?   northern/western
B. the ocean?   Atlantic
C. the sea?   Caribbean

Space 10: What is the name of . . .
A. both hemispheres?   northern/western
B. the ocean?   Atlantic
C. the gulf?   Gulf of Mexico

Space 11: What is the name of . . .
A. both hemispheres?   northern/western
B. the continent?   North America
C. the country?   Mexico

Space 12: What is the name of . . .
A. both hemispheres?   northern/western
B. the ocean?   Pacific
C. the gulf?   Gulf of California

Space 13: What is the name of . . .
A. both hemispheres?   northern/western
B. the continent?   North America
C. the river?   Mississippi River

Space 14: What is the name of . . .
A. both hemispheres?   northern/western
B. the continent?   North America
C. the mountains?   Rocky Mountains

Space 15: What is the name of . . .
A. both hemispheres?   northern/western
B. the ocean?   Pacific
C. the gulf?   Gulf of Alaska

Space 16: What is the name of . . .
A. both hemispheres?   northern/western
B. the continent?   North America
C. the imaginary line?   Arctic Circle

Space 17: What is the name of . . .
A. both hemispheres?   northern/western
B. the ocean?   Arctic
C. the sea?   Beaufort Sea

Space 18: What is the name of . . .
A. both hemispheres?   northern/western
B. the continent?   North America
C. the island?   Victoria Island

World Geography Game Question/Answer Sheet *(cont.)*

Space 19: What is the name of . . .
A. both hemispheres? northern/western
B. the continent? North America
C. the lakes? Great Lakes

Space 20: What is the name of . . .
A. both hemispheres? northern/western
B. the continent? North America
C. the bay? Hudson Bay

Space 21: What is the name of . . .
A. both hemispheres? northern/western
B. the continent? Antarctica
C. the island? Baffin Island

Space 22: What is the name of . . .
A. both hemispheres? northern/western
B. the continent? North America
C. the sea? Labrador Sea

Space 23: What is the name of . . .
A. both hemispheres? northern/western
B. the continent? North America
C. the island? Greenland

Space 24: What is the name of . . .
A. both hemispheres? northern/eastern
B. the continent? Europe
C. the island? Iceland

Space 25: What is the name of . . .
A. both hemispheres? northern/eastern
B. the continent? Europe
C. the peninsula? Ireland

Space 26: What is the name of . . .
A. both hemispheres? northern/eastern
B. the ocean? Atlantic
C. the sea? North Sea

Space 27: What is the name of . . .
A. both hemispheres? northern/eastern
B. the continent? Europe
C. the peninsula? Scandinavia

Space 28: What is the name of . . .
A. both hemispheres? northern/eastern
B. the ocean? Arctic
C. the sea? Barents Sea

Space 29: What is the name of . . .
A. both hemispheres? northern/eastern
B. the continent? Europe
C. the country? Russia

Space 30: What is the name of . . .
A. both hemispheres? northern/eastern
B. the continents? Europe and Asia
C. the mountains? Ural Mountains

Space 31: What is the name of . . .
A. both hemispheres? northern/eastern
B. the continent? Asia
C. the region? Siberia

Space 32: What is the name of . . .
A. both hemispheres? northern/eastern
B. the continent? Asia
C. the lake? Lake Baykal

Space 33: What is the name of . . .
A. both hemispheres? northern/eastern
B. the continent? Asia
C. the desert? Gobi Desert

Space 34: What is the name of . . .
A. both hemispheres? northern/eastern
B. the continent? Asia
C. the river? Huang Ho (Yellow R.)

Space 35: What is the name of . . .
A. both hemispheres? northern/eastern
B. the continent? Asia
C. the peninsula? Korean Peninsula

Space 36: What is the name of . . .
A. both hemispheres? northern/eastern
B. the continent? Asia
C. the island? Honshu

Space 37: What is the name of . . .
A. both hemispheres?   northern/eastern
B. the ocean?   Pacific
C. the sea?   East China Sea

Space 38: What is the name of . . .
A. both hemispheres?   northern/eastern
B. the continent?   Asia
C. the country?   China

Space 39: What is the name of . . .
A. both hemispheres?   northern/eastern
B. the continent?   Asia
C. the islands?   Philippine Islands

Space 40: What is the name of . . .
A. both hemispheres?   southern/eastern
B. the area?   Oceania
C. the island?   Borneo

Space 41: What is the name of . . .
A. both hemispheres?   southern/eastern
B. the continent?   Australia
C. the gulf?   Gulf of Carpentaria

Space 42: What is the name of . . .
A. both hemispheres?   southern/eastern
B. the area?   Oceania
C. the island?   New Guinea

Space 43: What is the name of . . .
A. both hemispheres?   southern/eastern
B. the continent?   Australia
C. the reef?   Great Barrier Reef

Space 44: What is the name of . . .
A. both hemispheres?   southern/eastern
B. the ocean?   Pacific
C. the sea?   Coral Sea

Space 45: What is the name of . . .
A. both hemispheres?   southern/eastern
B. the area?   Oceania
C. the country?   New Zealand

Space 46: What is the name of . . .
A. both hemispheres?   southern/eastern
B. the continent?   Australia
C. the island?   Tasmania

Space 47: What is the name of . . .
A. both hemispheres?   southern/eastern
B. the continent?   Australia
C. the country?   Australia

Space 48: What is the name of . . .
A. both hemispheres?   southern/eastern
B. the continent?   Asia
C. the island?   Java

Space 49: What is the name of . . .
A. both hemispheres?   southern/eastern
B. the continent?   Asia
C. the island?   Sumatra

Space 50: What is the name of . . .
A. both hemispheres?   northern/eastern
B. the continent?   Asia
C. the peninsula?   Indochina Peninsula

Space 51: What is the name of . . .
A. both hemispheres?   northern/eastern
B. the continent?   Asia
C. the bay?   Bay of Bengal

Space 52: What is the name of . . .
A. both hemispheres?   northern/eastern
B. the continent?   Asia
C. the mountains?   Himalayas

Space 53: What is the name of . . .
A. both hemispheres?   northern/eastern
B. the continent?   Asia
C. the country?   India

Space 54: What is the name of . . .
A. both hemispheres?   northern/eastern
B. the continents?   Europe and Asia
C. the sea?   Arabian Sea

Space 55: What is the name of . . .
A. both hemispheres?   northern/eastern
B. the continent?   Asia
C. the peninsula?   Arabian Peninsula

Space 56: What is the name of . . .
A. both hemispheres?   northern/eastern
B. the ocean?   Indian
C. the gulf?   Persian Gulf

Space 57: What is the name of . . .
A. both hemispheres?   northern/eastern
B. the continent?   Asia
C. the sea?   Caspian Sea

Space 58: What is the name of . . .
A. both hemispheres?   northern/eastern
B. the continent?   Asia
C. the desert?   Syrian Desert

Space 59: What is the name of . . .
A. both hemispheres?   northern/eastern
B. the continents?   Asia and Europe
C. the sea?   Black Sea

Space 60: What is the name of . . .
A. both hemispheres?   northern/eastern
B. the continent?   Europe
C. the plain?   Northern European
                              Plain

Space 61: What is the name of . . .
A. both hemispheres?   northern/eastern
B. the continent?   Europe
C. the mountains?   Alps

Space 62: What is the name of . . .
A. both hemispheres?   northern/eastern
B. the continent?   Europe
C. the peninsula?   Iberian Peninsula

Space 63: What is the name of . . .
A. both hemispheres?   northern/eastern
B. the ocean?   Atlantic
C. the sea?   Mediterranean

Space 64: What is the name of . . .
A. both hemispheres?   northern/eastern
B. the continent?   Africa
C. the desert?   Sahara Desert

Space 65: What is the name of . . .
A. both hemispheres?   northern/eastern
B. the continent?   Africa
C. the river?   Nile River

Space 66: What is the name of . . .
A. both hemispheres?   southern/eastern
B. the continent?   Africa
C. the sea?   Red Sea

Space 67: What is the name of . . .
A. both hemispheres?   southern/eastern
B. the continent?   Africa
C. the lake?   Lake Victoria

Space 68: What is the name of . . .
A. both hemispheres?   southern/eastern
B. the continent?   Africa
C. the island?   Madagascar

Space 69: What is the name of . . .
A. both hemispheres?   southern/eastern
B. the continent?   Africa
C. the cape?   The Cape of Good
                          Hope

Space 70: What is the name of . . .
A. both hemispheres?   southern/eastern
B. the continent?   Africa
C. the desert?   Kalahari Desert

Space 71: What is the name of . . .
A. both hemispheres?   southern/eastern
B. the continent?   Africa
C. the basin?   Congo Basin

Space 72: What is the name of . . .
A. both hemispheres?   southern/eastern
B. the ocean?   Atlantic
C. the gulf?   Gulf of Guinea

Idea Bank

Map Work

1. Have students outline the nations of the world, coloring and labeling them appropriately.
2. Have students mark significant physical features with symbols and label them on the maps provided.
3. Have students make raised relief maps of the continents, using plaster of Paris or a salt and flour mixture.
4. Give the students world maps and have them color and label the continents and oceans.
5. On a map of an ocean, have students plot and label significant features of the ocean floor.
6. Have students make specialty maps showing seasonal temperatures, precipitation, population distribution, major transportation routes, land use, etc.
7. Have students work in teams to divide the world map into time zones.

Continental Fair

Assign an inhabited continent to each of six groups. Have them organize booths and/or activities that reflect one or more cultures of their continents. The results might include food and food preparation, recordings of music, recordings of people speaking corresponding languages, folk dances, maps, charts, models, dioramas, products, crafts, artwork, pictures, or writings. Host a continental fair and invite parents or other classes to attend.

National Symbols

Have students recreate flags of the present and past, coats of arms, seals, and other symbols of the world's nations. Include brief descriptions of what the elements of each symbol represent and their significance to the nation's history or present time.

Idea Bank *(cont.)*

What's in the Media?

Have students collect and compile articles and pictures from newspapers and magazines that relate to people, countries, regions, or other areas within the continent being studied. Report about appropriate stories that appear on television news programs or in documentaries. Rent or borrow travel or documentary videos about world regions and view these in small groups or as a class. Make a recommended viewing list of appropriate feature films that are set in regions being studied.

Math Activities

Students can make horizontal or vertical bar graphs, picture graphs, or Venn diagrams comparing the populations, areas, highest mountains, etc., of the continents.

Compute differences among areas, populations, rural and urban populations, temperatures, etc., from data collected about the continents.

Guest Speakers

Involve the community as your students learn about world geography. Schedule guest speakers throughout the unit as a way of introducing students to a country or as part of a culminating activity. Try some of the following suggestions:

- Invite students, parents, or grandparents from different countries to share about their lives while living in those countries.
- Invite a member of a club or organization whose membership is composed of immigrants or their ancestors to share information and materials about their native lands.
- Write to embassies or consulates to obtain information about speakers or other resources.

Language Arts Activities

1. Select works of fiction that are set in foreign countries or assign the reading of such books to the students. Use any of a variety of reporting methods to share the stories. A selected bibliography is provided at the back of this book.

2. Have students create travel videos in which they share information about the continents they have studied.

3. Pretend to be one of the seven continents. Ask students to guess which continent you are by the continent clues that you give. You might also have them ask "Twenty Questions"-style questions.

The World

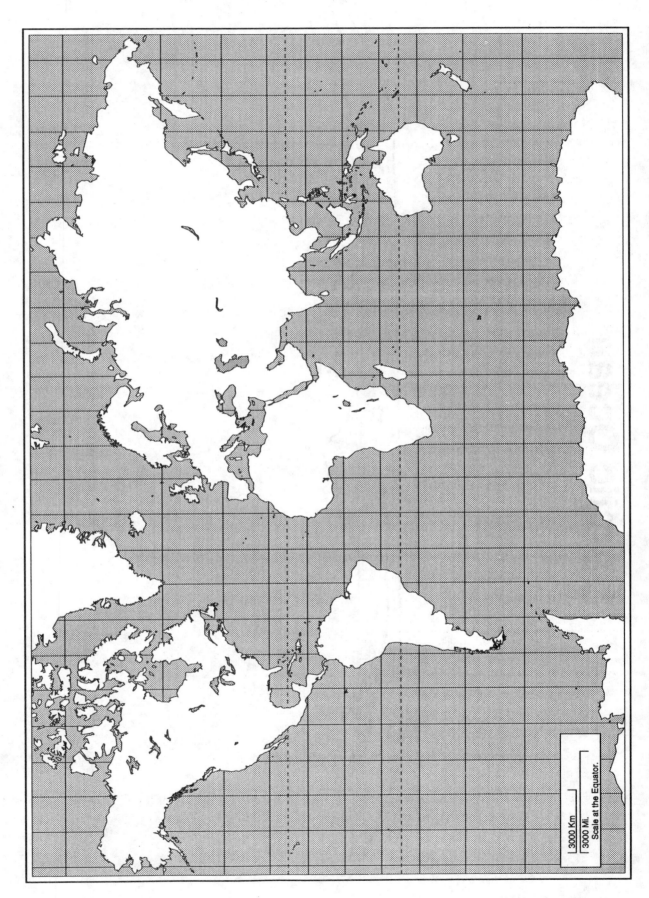

3000 Km
3000 Mi.
Scale at the Equator.

Arctic Ocean

Atlantic Ocean

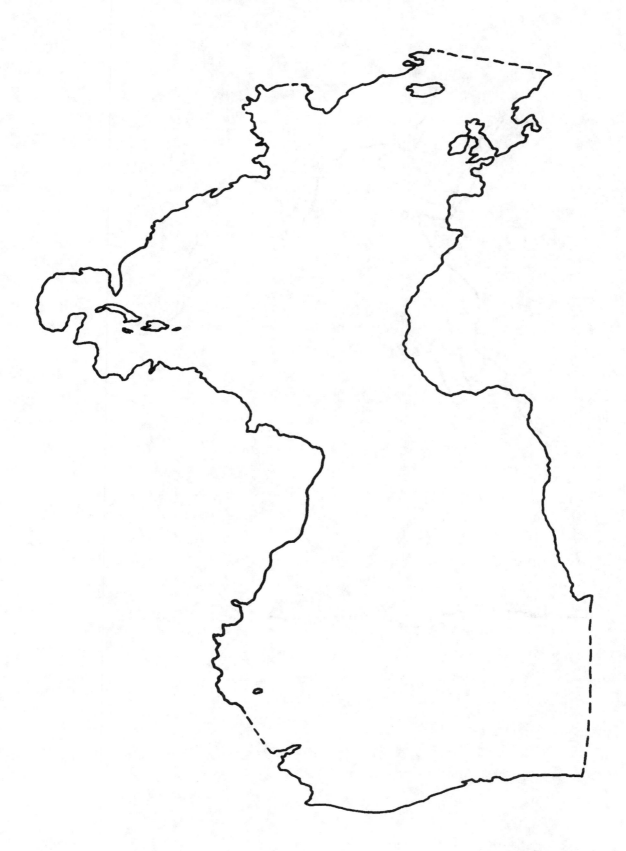

Indian Ocean

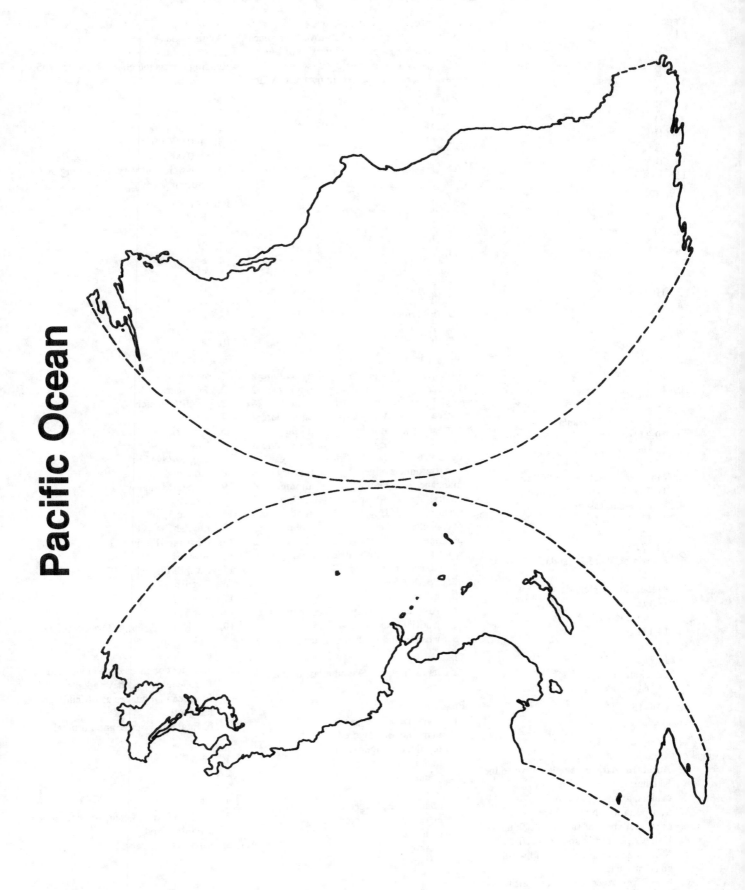

Pacific Ocean

Answer Key: Africa

Page 11
1. J
2. C
3. D
4. E
5. G
6. K
7. O
8. H
9. A
10. B
11. F
12. L
13. N
14. I
15. M

Page 12
1. D
2. F
3. H
4. G
5. B
6. C
7. J
8. A
9. E
10. I

Page 13
1. Kilimanjaro, Tanzania, 19,340
2. Kenya, Kenya, 17,058
3. Margherita Peak, Uganda-Zaire, 16,763
4. Ras Dashan, Ethiopia, 15,158
5. Meru, Tanzania, 14,979
6. Karisimbi, Zaire-Rwanda, 14,787
7. Elgon, Kenya-Uganda, 14,178
8. Batu, Ethiopia, 14,131
9. Gughe, Ethiopia, 13,780
10. Toubkal, Morocco, 13,661

Pages 14–15
See an atlas.

Page 16
For the map, see an atlas.
1. Bushmen: African people native to the Kalahari
2. camels: animals used for transportation in the Sahara
3. ergs: vast areas of sand in the Sahara
4. Kalahari: desert in southern Africa
5. Namib: desert along the southwest coast of Africa
6. Nile River: river that flows northward

through the eastern Sahara
7. nomads: people who move from place to place as part of their way of life (Bedouins in Sahara)
8. Sahara: huge desert in northern Africa

Page 17
1. I
2. H
3. C
4. J
5. F
6. A
7. G
8. K
9. D
10. B
11. E

Page 18
1. F
2. T
3. F (Tripoli)
4. F
5. T

Page 19

bananas	Uganda	agriculture	2
bauxite	Guinea	mining	2
coal	South Africa	mining	8
coffee	Ivory Coast	agriculture	4
copper	Zambia	mining	5
cotton	Egypt	agriculture	8
diamonds	South Africa	mining	1
forest products	Nigeria	forestry	8
manganese	Gabon	mining	4
natural gas	Algeria	mining	6
oranges	Egypt	agriculture	7
phosphate	Morocco	mining	7
uranium	South Africa	mining	2
wool	South Africa	agriculture	6

1. 10 (or 11 counting Ethiopia)
2. South Africa
3. mining
4. Answers will vary. Accept any justifiable answer.
5. western and southern Africa

Page 20
Answers will vary. See an atlas for the map.

Page 21
1. mammal, endangered
2. mammal, endangered
3. reptile, endangered
4. mammal
5. mammal
6. bird
7. mammal, endangered
8. mammal, endangered
9. mammal
10. mammal
11. mammal
12. mammal

13. bird
14. mammal
15. mammal
Reading across the chart: 9, 10, 15, 7, 5, 8, 13, 2, 11, 1, 12, 6, 14, 4, 3

Page 23
1. 290,000,000
2. 375,000,000
3. 490,000,000
4. 660,000,000
5. Answers will vary, depending on the current year.

Page 24
1. F
2. D
3. G
4. I
5. C
6. B
7. H
8. J
9. E
10. A

Page 25
1. Arabic
2. Portuguese
3. English/French
4. Arabic
5. Amharic
6. English
7. English/Swahili
8. Arabic
9. French/Malagasy
10. French
11. Arabic
12. English
13. Afrikaans/English
14. Arabic
15. Swahili/English
16. English
17. French
18. English
19. a. Algeria, Egypt, Libya, Morocco, and Sudan
    b. north
20. a. Some countries once controlled by European nations have adopted European languages as official languages.
    b. England, France, and Portugal

Page 26
1. 10%
2. Botswana
3. 40%
4. Islam
5. north and west: Islam; south, east, and central: mixed
6. Answers will vary.

Answer Key: Asia

Page 33
1. O
2. D
3. A
4. K
5. I
6. B
7. J
8. E
9. H
10. L
11. C
12. G
13. N
14. M
15. F

Page 34
1. D
2. G
3. I
4. E
5. J
6. C
7. H
8. A
9. F
10. B

Page 35
1. Everest, Nepal-Tibet, 29,028 feet/8,708 meters
2. K2-Godwin, Austen Kashmir 28,250
3. Kanchenjunga, India-Nepal, 28,208
4. Lhoste I, Nepal-Tibet, 27,923
5. Makalu I, Nepal-Tibet, 27,824
6. Lhotse II, Nepal-Tibet, 27,560
7. Dhaulagiri, Nepal, 26,810
8. Manaslu I, Nepal, 26,760
9. Cho Oyu, Nepal-Tibet, 26,750
10. Nanga Parbat, Kashmir, 26,660

Pages 36–37
See an atlas.

Page 38
For the map, see an atlas.
1. Gobi: desert in southern Mongolia and northern China.
2. camels: humped animals used for transportation; Bactrian when found in Mongolia and Arabian in Arabia
3. Bedouin: nomadic people of Middle Eastern deserts
4. Karakum: large desert in Turkmen
5. Kyzyl-Kum: desert southeast of the Aral Sea in southern Kazakhstan and northern Uzbekistan
6. Rub al Khali: huge desert in southern Saudi Arabia
7. Taklimakan: desert in northwestern China
8. yurts: collapsible, felt-covered tents of Mongolia

Page 39
1. F
2. L
3. C
4. I
5. O
6. A
7. G
8. M
9. D
10. J
11. K
12. B
13. H
14. N
15. E

Page 40
1. T
2. F (Teheran)
3. T
4. F (The reason is not clear from the graphs.)
5. F (Shanghai, Tokyo, and Teheran have growing seasons shorter than twelve months).

Page 41

bananas	India	agriculture	3
bauxite	Russia	mining	1
coal	China	mining	2
coffee	Indonesia	agriculture	3
copper	Russia	mining	4
cotton	China	agriculture	1
forest products	Russia	forestry	2
iron	Russia	mining	1
rice	China	agriculture	1
rubber	Malaysia	agriculture	1
soybeans	China	agriculture	3
tin	Malaysia	mining	1
tuna	Japan	fishing	1
wheat	China	agriculture	1

1. six
2. China
3. agriculture
4. Answers will vary. Accept any justifiable answer.
5. eastern and southern Asia

Page 42
Answers will vary. See an atlas for the map.

Page 43
1. mammal, endangered
2. mammal, endangered
3. mammal
4. mammal, endangered
5. mammal, endangered
6. bird
7. mammal
8. reptile
9. mammal
10. mammal
11. mammal
12. bird
13. mammal
14. mammal
15. mammal, endangered
Reading across the chart: 6, 7, 1, 3, 14, 15, 2, 4, 8, 5, 10, 11, 9, 12, 13

Page 45
1. 1,700,000,000
2. 2,100,000,000
3. 2,600,000,000
4. 3,100,000,000
5. Answers will vary.
6. Answers will vary, depending on the current year.

Page 46
1. F
2. C
3. B
4. I
5. E
6. A
7. H
8. D
9. J
10. G

Page 47
1. Bengali
2. Khmer
3. Chinese
4. Hindi/English
5. Indonesian
6. Arabic
7. Hebrew
8. Japanese
9. Arabic
10. Korean
11. Malay
12. Urdu
13. Filipino/English
14. Russian
15. Arabic
16. Arabic
17. Thai
18. Turkish
19. Vietnamese
20. a. Iraq, Jordan, Saudi Arabia, and Syria
    b. west
21. twelve

Page 48
1. 97.5%
2. Philippines
3. 92.5%
4. Islam
5. Buddhism is not popular in India today.
6. Answers will vary.

Answer Key: Australia and Oceania

Page 55
1. C
2. M
3. D
4. J
5. K
6. E
7. G
8. F
9. H
10. A
11. B
12. L
13. N
14. I
15. O

Page 56
1. F
2. C
3. J
4. H
5. E
6. B
7. G
8. A
9. D
10. I

Page 57
1. Java, New Guinea. 16,500
2. Trikora, New Guinea, 15,585
3. Mandala, New Guinea, 15,420
4. Wilhelm, Papua, New Guinea, 14,793
5. Mauna Kea, United States, 13,796
6. Mauna Loa, United States, 13,677
7. Cook, New Zealand, 12,349
8. Kosciusko, Australia, 7,310

Pages 58–59
See an atlas.

Page 60
For the map, see an atlas.
1. Simpson Desert: desert in central Australia
2. Great Victoria Desert: large desert in southern Australia
3. Great Sandy Desert: large desert in northwest Australia
4. Ayers Rock: huge rock in central Australia
5. Aborigines: native Australian desert inhabitants
6. Alice Springs: remote central-Australian town
7. red kangaroo: marsupial common to Australian deserts
8. outback: slang term for interior region, including deserts

Page 61
1. H
2. C
3. I

4. B
5. F
6. L
7. D
8. J
9. A
10. G
11. K
12. E

Page 62
1. F
2. T
3. T
4. F
5. Sydney and Auckland lie below the equator, so their seasons are reversed from the northern hemisphere.

Page 63

wool	Australia	agriculture	1
bauxite	Australia	mining	1
coal	Australia	mining	9
coconuts	New Guinea	agriculture	5
copper	Australia	mining	9
gold	Australia	mining	7
iron	Australia	mining	3
nickel	Australia	mining	3
oats	Australia	agriculture	8
silver	Australia	mining	6
sugar	Australia	agriculture	7
tin	Australia	mining	8
tungsten	Australia	mining	5
uranium	Australia	mining	4
wheat	Australia	agriculture	8

1. two
2. Australia
3. mining
4. Australia seems to be wealthiest because it appears to have the most mineral wealth.
5. the western region

Page 64
Answers will vary. See an atlas for the map.

Page 65
1. mammal
2. bird
3. mammal
4. bird
5. mammal
6. bird
7. bird
8. mammal
9. bird
10. bird
11. mammal
12. mammal
13. mammal
14. mammal
15. mammal
Reading across the chart: 2, 14, 15, 7, 11, 10, 3, 6, 8, 4, 13, 9, 5, 1, 12

Page 67
1. 29,000,000
2. 34,000,000
3. 41,000,000
4. 46,000,000
5. Answers will vary.
6. Answers will vary, depending on the current year.

Page 68
1. G
2. I
3. C
4. E
5. B
6. H
7. F
8. A
9. D
10. J

Page 69
1. English
2. English
3. English
4. English
5. English
6. Nauruan
7. English
8. English
9. English/Melanesian
10. Tongan/English
11. Tuvaluan/English
12. English/Bislama
13. Samoan/English
14. a. Samoan/English
    b. United States
15. a. French
    b. France
16. a. English
    b. Australia
17. a. French
    b. France
18. a. English
    b. United Kingdom

Page 70
1. a. Guam
    b. Kiribati
2. a. yes
    b. There are many Catholics and Protestants there now.
3. a. no
    b. They are not represented on the graph.
4. Answers will vary.

Answer Key: Europe

Page 77
1. I
2. K
3. A
4. L
5. B
6. J
7. F
8. D
9. G
10. O
11. C
12. H
13. E
14. N
15. M

Page 78
1. I
2. J
3. E
4. B
5. H
6. D
7. G
8. C
9. A
10. F

Page 79
1. Mont Blanc, France-Italy 15,771
2. Monte Rosa, Switzerland 15,203
3. Dom, Switzerland 14,911
4. Liskamm, Italy-Switzerland 14,852
5. Weisshorn, Switzerland 14,780
6. Taschhorn, Switzerland 14,733
7. Matterhorn, Italy-Switzerland 14,690
8. Dent Blanche, Switzerland 14,293
9. Nadelhorn, Switzerland 14,196
10. Grand Combin, Switzerland 14,154

Pages 80–81
See an atlas.

Page 82
For the map, see an atlas.
1. Astrakhan: largest desert city in Europe
2. caviar: egg food from sturgeon
3. Caspian Sea: body of water bordering the desert
4. Volga River: flows through the desert and empties into the Caspian Sea
5. Caspian Depression: lowland bordering the Caspian Sea

6. Ryn-Peski: sandy region of the Caspian Depression
7. Ural River: eastern border of the European part of the desert
8. sturgeon: caviar-producing fish found in the Caspian Sea

Page 83
1. F
2. L
3. N
4. H
5. B
6. J
7. A
8. G
9. E
10. K
11. C
12. M
13. I
14. O
15. D

Page 84
1. F (Rome/Moscow)
2. F (Moscow)
3. T
4. T
5. F (only Rome/Athens)

Page 85

cattle	France	agriculture	10
coal	Germany	mining	3
copper	Poland	mining	8
grapes	France	agriculture	1
iron	Sweden	mining	9
natural gas	Netherlands	mining	3
oats	Russia	agriculture	1
petroleum	Great Britain	mining	5
potatoes	Poland	agriculture	2
rye	Poland	agriculture	1
sugar beets	Ukraine	agriculture	1
tin	Great Britain	mining	9
tungsten	Austria	mining	7
wheat	France	agriculture	5

1. nine
2. France and Poland
3. agriculture and mining
4. Answers will vary.
5. There is no concentration.

Page 86
Answers will vary. See an atlas for the map.

Page 87
1. reptile
2. mammal
3. mammal
4. mammal
5. bird
6. mammal
7. fish
8. mammal

9. bird
10. mammal
11. bird
12. mammal
13. bird
14. fish
15. mammal
Reading across the chart: 4, 12, 6, 1, 8, 7, 3, 15, 5, 10, 9, 14, 11, 2, 13

Page 89
1. 585,000,000
2. 645,000,000
3. 685,000,000
4. 715,000,000
5. Answers will vary.
6. Answers will vary, depending on the current year.

Page 90
1. J
2. C
3. H
4. A
5. F
6. E
7. B
8. I
9. G
10. D

Page 91
1. German
2. Flemish/French
3. Finnish/Swedish
4. French
5. German
6. Greek
7. Italian
8. Lithuanian
9. Norwegian
10. Polish
11. Portuguese
12. Romanian/Hungarian/German
13. Russian
14. Spanish
15. Swedish
16. German/French/Italian
17. Ukrainian
18. English/Gaelic
19. a. German
    b. Austria, Germany, Romania, and Switzerland
    c. spread throughout the southwest quadrant
20. Italian, French, Spanish, Portuguese, and Romanian

Page 92
1. 90%
2. Germany
3. 5%
4. Answers will vary.
5. Answers will vary.

Answer Key: North America

Page 99
1. F
2. M
3. J
4. B
5. E
6. D
7. K
8. I
9. A
10. O
11. N
12. H
13. G
14. C
15. L

Page 100
1. I
2. C
3. B
4. F
5. E
6. G
7. H
8. J
9. D
10. A

Page 101
1. McKinley, United States, 20,320
2. Logan, Canada, 19,850
3. Citlaltepec, Mexico, 18,700
4. St. Elias, United States-Canada 18,008
5. Popocatepétl, Mexico, 17,887
6. Foraker, United States, 17,400
7. Iztaccihuatl, Mexico, 17,343
8. Lucania, Canada, 17,147
9. King, Canada, 16,971
10. Steele, Canada, 16,644

Pages 102–103
See an atlas.

Page 104
For the map, see an atlas.
1. Baja, California: peninsula that is almost entirely desert
2. Colorado River: flows through desert of southwestern United States
3. coyote: mammal of canine family found in deserts
4. Death Valley: lowest point in North America (in the Mojave Desert)
5. Great Basin: desert area covering much of Nevada
6. Great Salt Lake: large salty lake in the Utah desert
7. Mojave Desert: desert in southwestern United States (California and Arizona)
8. Painted Desert: area of colorful desert land in Arizona

Page 105
1. D
2. F
3. K
4. B
5. J
6. I
7. A
8. E
9. H
10. N
11. G
12. C
13. L
14. O
15. M

Page 106
1. F (Havana and Montreal)
2. T
3. T
4. F (temperature)
5. F (Los Angeles, Havana, and Mexico City)

Page 107

bauxite	Jamaica	mining	4
cattle	United States	agriculture	3
coal	United States	mining	1
copper	United States	mining	2
cotton	United States	agriculture	2
forest prodts.	United States	forestry	2
iron	United States	mining	5
natural gas	United States	mining	1
oats	United States	agriculture	2
oranges	United States	agriculture	2
petroleum	United States	mining	2
sugar beets	United States	agriculture	3
tungsten	Canada	mining	3
uranium	Canada	mining	1
wheat	United States	agriculture	3

1. three
2. United States
3. mining
4. United States (Accept any justifiable answer.)
5. northern

Page 108
Answers will vary. See an atlas for the map.

Page 109
1. mammal
2. bird
3. mammal
4. mammal
5. mammal
6. reptile
7. mammal
8. mammal
9. mammal
10. mammal
11. mammal
12. bird

13. reptile
14. mammal
15. mammal
Reading across the chart: 15, 12, 11, 6, 9, 10, 4, 14, 2, 13, 7, 1, 3, 5, 8

Page 111
1. 270,000,000
2. 320,000,000
3. 375,000,000
4. 425,000,000
5. Answers will vary.
6. Answers will vary depending on the current year.

Page 112
1. A
2. H
3. F
4. E
5. J
6. I
7. C
8. D
9. B
10. G

Page 113
1. English
2. English
3. English
4. English
5. English/French
6. Spanish
7. Spanish
8. English
9. Spanish
10. Spanish
11. Spanish
12. French
13. Spanish
14. English
15. Spanish
16. Spanish
17. Spanish
18. English
19. a. Costa Rica, Cuba, Dominican Republic, El Salvador, Guatemala, Honduras, Mexico, Nicaragua, and Panama
    b. southern
20. a. They speak European languages.
    b. Great Britain, France, and Spain

Page 114
1. 40%
2. United States
3. 50%
4. Catholic
5. Responses will vary.

Answer Key: South America

Page 121
1. D
2. E
3. F
4. I
5. O
6. M
7. B
8. G
9. A
10. C
11. J
12. H
13. L
14. K
15. N

Page 122
1. B
2. G
3. D
4. A
5. F
6. H
7. J
8. C
9. E
10. I

Page 123
1. Aconcagua, Argentina, 22,834
2. Ojos del Salado, Argentina-Chile 22,572
3. Bonete, Argentina, 22,546
4. Tupungato, Argentina-Chile, 22,310
5. Pissis, Argentina , 22,241
6. Mercedario, Argentina, 22,211
7. Huascaran, Peru, 22,205
8. Llullaillaco, Argentina-Chile, 22,057
9. El Libertador, Argentina, 22,047
10. Cachi, Argentina, 22,047

Pages 124–125
See an atlas.

Page 126
For the map, see an atlas.
1. Atacama: very dry desert along the Pacific coast
2. Andes Mountains: mountain range bordering both deserts of South America
3. copper: metal mined in the Atacama region
4. Loa River: river that passes through the Atacama Desert
5. Patagonia: desert in southeast South America
6. Sechura: Chilean name for the Atacama region
7. sheep: animal raised in Patagonia
8. sodium nitrate: mineral found in Atacama

Page 127
1. L
2. B
3. D
4. H
5. G
6. A
7. C
8. I
9. F
10. J
11. K
12. E

Page 128
1. F (São Paolo, Buenos Aires)
2. F (Buenos Aires)
3. T
4. F (similar temperatures only)
5. F (all but La Paz)

Page 129

bananas	Brazil	agriculture	1
bauxite	Brazil	mining	4
cattle	Brazil	agriculture	2
coffee	Brazil	agriculture	1
copper	Chile	mining	1
fish	Chile	fishing	5
forest products	Brazil	forestry	3
gold	Brazil	mining	5
iron ore	Brazil	mining	2
lead	Peru	mining	5
manganese	Brazil	mining	3
sugar cane	Brazil	agriculture	1
tin	Brazil	mining	4
wool	Argentina	agriculture	5

1. four
2. Brazil
3. mining
4. Brazil (Accept any reasonable answer.)
5. Accept any reasonable answer.

Page 130
Answers will vary. See an atlas for the map.

Page 131
1. bird
2. mammal
3. mammal
4. mammal
5. mammal
6. mammal, endangered
7. mammal
8. reptile, endangered
9. mammal
10. bird
11. bird
12. mammal
13. mammal
14. mammal

15. reptile
Reading across the chart: 1, 6, 2, 9, 10, 14, 11, 15, 13, 7, 12, 4, 5, 3, 8

Page 133
1. 145,000,000
2. 190,000,000
3. 240,000,000
4. 300,000,000
5. Responses will vary.
6. Answers will vary, depending on the current year.

Page 134
1. F
2. I
3. A
4. H
5. K
6. M
7. C
8. L
9. D
10. J
11. E
12. G
13. B

Page 135
1. Spanish
2. Spanish/Aymara/Quechua
3. Portuguese
4. Spanish
5. Spanish
6. Spanish/Quechua
7. English
8. Spanish/Guarani
9. Spanish/Quechua
10. Dutch
11. Spanish
12. Spanish
13. a. English
    b. United Kingdom
14. a. French
    b. France
15. a. Spanish
    b. north, west, and south
16. a. They speak European languages.
    b. Spain, France, Netherlands, Portugal, and Great Britain

Page 136
1. 10%
2. Colombia
3. 12.5%
4. Catholic

Answer Key: Antarctica

Page 143
1. I
2. C
3. A
4. F
5. E
6. H
7. J
8. D
9. L
10. K
11. B
12. G

Page 144
1. Vinson Massif, 16,864
2. Tyree, 16,290
3. Shinn, 15,750
4. Gardner, 15,375
5. Epperly, 15,100
6. Kirkpatrick, 14,855
7. Elizabeth, 14,698
8. Markham, 14,290
9. Bell, 14,117
10. Mackellar, 14,098

Pages 145–146
See an atlas.

Page 147
1. B
2. E
3. D
4. F
5. A
6. C
7. G
8. H

Page 148

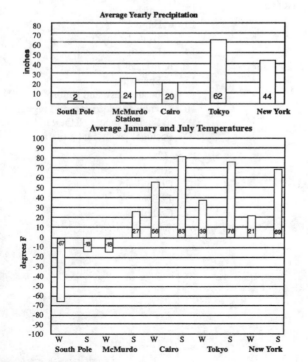

Page 149
1. bird
2. bird
3. mammal, endangered
4. bird
5. mammal
6. bird
7. bird
8. mammal
9. mammal
10. mammal
11. bird
12. mammal
13. bird
14. mammal
15. mammal

Reading across the chart: 6, 3, 2, 12, 1, 4, 5, 10, 7, 9, 13, 15, 8, 11, 14

Resources

Three types of references are very helpful for students working with the activities in this book: atlases, encyclopedias, and world almanacs. Having available at least one set of recent encyclopedias for the entire class to share and an atlas and almanac for every four students would be particularly beneficial. Some of the more useful sources are listed below.

Classroom Atlas. Rand McNally & Company.

Follett Student Atlas. Follett Publishing Company, Chicago.

Wright, John W. (general editor). *The Universal Almanac.* Andrews and McMeel, Kansas City.

The World Almanac and Book of Facts. Newspaper Enterprise Association, New York.

World Atlas. Nystrom, Chicago.

The World Book Encyclopedia. World Book, Inc., Chicago.

Bibliography

Africa

Aardema, Verna. *Why Mosquitoes Buzz in People's Ears.* (Dial, 1975).

Bertol, Roland. *Sundiata: The Epic of the Lion King.* (Crowell, 1970).

Cendrars, Blaise. *Shadow.* (Scribner, 1982).

Courlander, Harold. *The King's Drum and Other African Tales.* (Harcourt, 1962).

El-Shamy, Hasan. *Folktales of Egypt.* (University of Chicago Press, 1980).

Pitcher, Diana. *Tokoloshi.* (Celestial Arts, 1981).

Asia

Sadler, Catherine. *Treasure Mountain: Folktales from Southern China.* (Atheneum, 1982).

Tehranchian, Hassan. *Kalilah and Dimnah: Fables from the Middle East.* (Harmony, 1985).

Thompson, Brian. *The Story of Prince Rama.* (Viking, 1985).

Travers, P.L. *Two Pairs of Shoes.* (Atheneum, 1980).

Australia and Oceania

Sperry, Armstrong. *Call It Courage.* (Macmillan, 1940).

Williams, Jay. *The Surprising Things Maui Did.* (Four Winds, 1979).

Europe

Andersen, Hans Christian (translation by Erik Christian Haugaard). *The Complete Fairy Tales and Stories.* (Doubleday, 1974).

Asbjornsen, Peter C. and Jorgen Moe. *East of the Sun and West of the Moon.* (Macmillan, 1963).

Dejong, Meindert. *The Wheel on the School.* (Harper, 1954).

Dickens, Charles. *A Christmas Carol.* (Lippincott, 1966).

Grimm, Jakob and Wilhelm. *The Complete Fairy Tales.* (Panteon, 1974).

Nic Leodhas, Sorche. *By Loch and Lin: Tales from Scottish Ballads.* (Holt, 1976).

Perrault, Charles. *Perrault's Complete Fairy Tales.* (Dodd, 1961).

Seredy, Kate. *The Good Master.* (Viking, 1961).

Singer, Isaac Bashevis. *The Fearsome Inn.* (Scribner, 1967).

North America

Belpre, Pura. *Santiago.* (Warner, 1969).

Hamilton, Virginia. *The People Could Fly.* (Knopf, 1985).

Harris, Christie. *Once Upon a Totem.* (Atheneum, 1967).

Houston, James. *Akavak: An Eskimo Journey.* (Harcourt, 1968).

South America

Bierhorst, John. *Black Rainbow: Legends of the Incas & Myths of Ancient Peru.* (Farrar, Strauss, & Giroux, Inc., 1976.)

Clark, Ann Nolan. *Secret of the Andes.* (Viking, 1952).

Cohen, Miriam. *Born to Dance Samba.* (HarperC Child Bks., 1984).

Cosgrove, Stephen. *Pish-Posh.* (Price Stern, 1986).

O'Dell, Scott. *The Amethyst Ring.* (Houghton, Mifflin Co., 1983).

Bibliography *(cont.)*

Technology

Broderbund. *MacGlobe & PC Globe and MacUSA & PC USA.* Available from Learning Services, (800) 877-9378. disk

Broderbund. *Where in the World Is Carmen Sandiego?* Available from Troll (800)526-5289. CD-ROM and disk

Bureau of Electronic Publishing Inc. *World Fact Book.* Available from Educational Resources, (800)624-2926. CD-ROM

DeLorme Publishing. *Global Explorer.* Available from DeLorme Publishing, 1995. CD-ROM

Discis. *Great Cities of the World, Volumes 1 & 2.* Available from Learning Services, (800)877-9378. CD-ROM

Impressions. *My First World Atlas.* Available from Educational Resources, (800)624-2926.

Lawrence. *Nigel's World Adventures in World Geography.* Available from Educational Resources, (800)624-2926. CD-ROM and disk

Macmillan/McGraw-Hill. *World Atlas Action.* Available from Learning Services, (800)877-9378. disk

Magic Quest. *Time Treks and Earth Treks.* Available from Educational Resources, (800)624-2926. disk

MECC. *The Amazon Trail, Canada Geograph II, The Oregon Trail, The Yukon Trail, and USA Geograph II.* Available from MECC, (800)685-MECC; in Canada call (800)663-7731. CD-ROM and disk

Mindscape. *World Atlas.* Available from Educational Resources, (800)624-2926. disk

National Geographic. *Picture Atlas of the World.* Available from Educational Resources, (800)624-2926. CD-ROM

National Geographic. *Rain Forest and Zip Zap Map.* Available from Educational Resources, (800)624-2926. laserdisc and disk

National Geographic. *STV: World Geography.* Available from National Geographic Educational Technology, (800)368-2728. videodisc

Newton Technology. *GEOvista Tutor.* Available from William K. Bradford, (800)421-2009. disk

Orange Cherry. *Time Traveler.* Available from Educational Resources, (800)624-2926. CD-ROM

Pride in Learning. *Global Issues.* Available from Educational Resources (800)624-2926. disk

Queue. *Atlas Explorer.* Available from Educational Resources, (800)624-2926. disk

Sanctuary Woods. *Ecology Treks.* Available from Learning Services, (800)877-3278. software and videodisc

Software Toolworks. *World Atlas. Available from Learning Services, (800)877-9378. CD-ROM and disk*

SVE. *Geography on Laserdisc.* Available from Learning Services, (800)877-9378. laserdisc

Virigin Sound & Vision. *One Tribe and One World Atlas.* Available from Educational Resources, (800)624-2926. CD-ROM